Bounds Out of Bounds

Bounds
Out of Bounds

A Compass for Recent
American and British Poetry

Roberta Berke

New York
OXFORD UNIVERSITY PRESS
1981

Copyright © 1981 by Roberta Berke

Library of Congress Cataloging in Publication Data

Berke, Roberta Elzey.
    Bounds out of bounds.

    Includes bibliographical references and index.
    1. American poetry—20th century—History and
criticism.   2. English poetry—20th century—History
and criticism.   I. Title.
PS323.5.B4   821'.91'09   80-20886
ISBN 0-19-502872-4

Printed in the United States of America

Preface

Anyone who would be a poet beyond his twenty-fifth year must have a historical sense, said T. S. Eliot. When faced with an impasse in my own work, I realized that in addition to a historical sense I would have to develop a contemporary sense. So I began to read or re-read all the poets who had become well known since 1950 and soon wondered why I liked certain poems better than others, and what makes a good poem. It was obvious that some poets' reputations were based on their membership in certain cliques which waged vitriolic war on other cliques. I had to discover a way of assessing poetry that went beyond literary gangs or momentary responses and which was valid for and tolerant of a wide variety of styles. Each group of poets held discoveries and disappointments and each group had something different and fresh to teach about writing poetry. The newer poets in particular have convinced me that it is now possible to write poetry that goes beyond the bounds of styles, subjects or personal stereotypes.

Although my main reason for embarking on this study of contemporary poetry was personal, in my judgments I have tried to represent objectively a wide readership. Specialists and connoisseurs of critical conundrums will have to be patient or go elsewhere, for I intend to present poets as clearly as possible for the man in the library, if not for the man in the street. This doesn't mean that contemporary poetry is simple and easy to understand—far from it. But neither is poetry merely a pretext for critics to show off by superimposing as elaborate a structure of their own as possible on it. In particular I would like to demonstrate to younger poets what is being done now and how it might relate to their own work in progress. I hope that readers will become as excited and encouraged as I have by the new possibilities in poetry today.

I could not have written this book without many kinds of help from many different people. My children, Joshua and Deborah, with a tolerance beyond their years, accepted that I was often tired, preoccupied and downright crabby. My husband, Joseph, endured all this plus night after night of casseroles cremated in the red pot. Three librarians have aided me far beyond the call of duty: Jonathan Barker of the Arts Council Poetry Library in London, Alex Gildzen of the Special Collections at Kent State University in Ohio and Geoffrey Soar of the University College Library in London. Nothing was too obscure for them: if a poem had been published on tissue paper in Ashtabula, Ohio, in 1953 they could locate a copy; if a poet lived in a shack in the Himalayas they could scent him out and provide his address and bibliography. The staff at the London Library also lived up to their well-deserved reputation for helpfulness. The newer poets in Chapter Nine have very generously sent me books, entrusted me with manuscripts and taken time to put on paper their ideas about poetry. I am indebted to the editors of *The Ardis Anthology of New American Poetry* for providing me with addresses of some poets and for their wide-ranging selection. Edward Field's recent anthology, *A Geography of Poets*, has also been useful to me. Asa Benveniste spent many hours talking with me about his experiences as a poetry publisher. I am grateful to the University of Copenhagen, which invited me to give a lecture upon which this book was later based, and to A. Alvarez and Frank Kermode, who generously listened to it. Kent State University also invited me to lecture on contemporary poetry.

My editor, James Raimes, has been enthusiastic and patient even when it looked like I would not be finished before Oxford University Press's second 500th birthday. His astute influence has reeled in the book whenever it appeared to be veering out of bounds. Sheldon Meyer, Senior Vice President of Oxford University Press, made time in his busy schedule to complete the editorial work and see this book through the press. Stephanie Golden, Associate Editor, wrestled to translate into readable English my erratic spelling and some poets' eccentric typography. I am also very grateful to my intrepid agents —Pat Kavanagh, Victoria Pryor, and Joan Fulton—for their energy and advice.

My heartfelt thanks to all of them.

R.B.

Primrose Hill, London
May 1980

Contents

[The artist] strives not for a disintegration of syntax but for a complication within syntax, overlapping structures, so that words are freed, having bounds out of bound[s].

Robert Duncan, *Bending the Bow*

Bounds Out of Bounds

1

It's Time
to Ask Questions

". . . Writing a book on contemporary poetry," I replied to the usual "what do you do" question. Harry looked as embarrassed as if I had said "contemporary pornography" and stared at the melting ice in his glass. "I'm afraid I don't read poetry any more," he confessed, then brightened: "But I *used* to read it and buy small press books and go to readings. I don't know why I lost interest. . . ."

You and a lot of others, Harry: intelligent, literate people, young, old and middle-aged, have largely given up the struggle to enjoy and understand the poetry that is being written right now. Poetry has become more accessible yet more remote than ever before. Myriad small presses make a bewildering variety of poets available in formats ranging from elegant limited editions that integrate artwork and text to photocopied chapbooks which are often given away. Since 1950 little magazines have increased their numbers by 1,000 percent[1] and have an influence far beyond what their small circulation figures would suggest, because their editors publish what they like, rather than what will please the public and sell. Before, poets might circulate manuscripts among friends; now they frequently publish in little magazines which serve the same purpose.[2] This expansion of poetry presses and magazines has been aided by new technology that now enables almost anyone to print a book almost as easily as mimeographing the PTA newsletter. There has also been a growth in the number of university students, and more universities have sponsored literary quarterlies. Grants have become available, not only for magazines, but also for poets in residence and newly popular poetry readings. Poetry has also become decentralized since the early seventies; no longer is it vital to be part of a big-city "scene" to be published.

Suddenly you can say anything. This general overthrow of inhibitions and release of the strictures of literary criticism in particular is the most important cause of the recent explosion of poetry. Sex, politics and race are now not merely possible subjects for some poets, but obligatory concerns. Even if the majority of poets are not so flamboyant as the circuit stars, many have exposed their personal lives much more openly in their poems than ever before. Yet all this openness, this discarding of rules, has not made contemporary poetry any easier to understand. For, at the same time, the general movement of modern poetry away from narrative has now been extended by some poets to a movement away from any meaning at all. Words are often presented for their own sake rather than in a logical sequence intended for communication; in Concrete Poetry the words become visual objects in pictorial typography. The barriers separating the art forms have been broken down. Music is now blended with poetry in mixtures ranging from reading to a jazz background, to writing and singing rock music, to sound poetry—tones and syllables performed by the poet and not reproducible on the page.

No wonder many readers, like Harry, feel confused about and remote from the flurry of poetry going on around them. As the eighties begin, it's time to ask some hard, basic questions about poetry. Why do we prefer some poems to others? How do we decide what makes a good poem? The staggering amount of poetry published today means that the reader must select more actively and strenuously than ever before.

Can we apply any rules when making our choice of contemporary poetry without imposing "normality" and stifling experiment? Will the diverse poets active at the moment fit into any Procrustean set of standards? Although we are concerned today to assess poems without imposing artificial restrictions, this problem is not a new one; the search for criteria has been going on for a long time. For Aristotle poetry was an imitation, and the form of poetry had to reflect the wholeness of the object or action imitated.[3] The methods of technical analysis which Aristotle devised were used by critics for centuries afterwards. In Elizabethan times, Sir Philip Sidney added an end purpose to poetry: pleasing and thereby morally instructing an audience. This could be achieved, according to John Dryden in the seventeenth century, by following a set of rules: "Having thus shewn that imitation pleases, and why it pleases in both these arts, it follows that some rules of imitation are necessary to obtain the end; for without rules there can be no art, any more than there can be a house without a door to conduct you into it."[4] Although Samuel Johnson did not evolve any new critical theory, his "common-sense" discussions of Shakespeare and many other poets set an example for later critics.

A decisive break with this Aristotelian tradition came in 1800 in Wordsworth's Preface to his *Lyrical Ballads*: "Poetry is the spontaneous overflow of powerful feelings: it takes its origin from emotion recollected in tranquility: the emotion is contemplated til, by a species of reaction, the tranquility gradually disappears, and an emotion, kindred to that which was before the subject of contemplation, is gradually produced, and does itself actually exist in the mind."[5] Similar beliefs were held by other Romantic poets—Keats, Shelley, Blake and particularly Coleridge, whose profound exploration of the poet's consciousness, *Biographia Literaria*, appeared in 1817. Aristotle's imitation of external reality had been replaced by expression of the poet's inner emotions as the touchstone by which poetry was judged. The French Symbolist poets saw themselves as visionaries whose Promethean task was to discover through their sensibilities the eternity underlying apparent reality and to seek in the "forest of symbols" we wander through every day an image that would re-evoke that insight.[6] The Symbolists' concept of poetry as a means toward transcending ordinary consciousness has continued to influence later poets, particularly those writing today.

Another view of poetry sees the poem as a world of its own, an object whose existence does not need to be justified by purposes such as delight, moral instruction or even meaning. This concept, loosely termed "art for art's sake," began to develop in the late eighteenth and early nineteenth centuries out of Kant's formula that a work of art ought to show intention without tendentiousness. This idea that a poem exists in its own right underlies the Modernists' free-verse revolt against Victorian verbosity and sentiment, and prompted the Imagists' 1912 tenets: "1. Direct treatment of the 'thing' whether subjective or objective. 2. To use absolutely no word which does not contribute to the presentation. 3. As regarding rhythm: to compose in the sequence of the musical phrase, not in the sequence of the metronome."[7] "Objective Criticism" became the dogma of the New Critics such as T. S. Eliot, I. A. Richards, William Empson, John Crowe Ransom, Allen Tate and Robert Penn Warren. Archibald MacLeish's "Ars Poetica" was widely quoted: "A poem should be palpable and mute / As a globed fruit. . . . / A poem should not mean / But be."[8] The later New Critics strafed such limping stragglers of Romanticism and Symbolism as "The Intentional Fallacy" (confusion between the poem and its origins). The New Critics made criticism into a growth industry, earnestly labeled by Ransom "Criticism Inc." New Critical ideas were employed most eloquently by Wallace Stevens as he created a complex kingdom of the imagination, "a supreme fiction," in poems such as "The Idea of Order at Key West": ". . . there never was a world for her / Except the one she sang, and, singing, made."[9]

Since the early sixties the French Structuralist critics have been influential among academic critics, but not among poets. Drawing upon the linguistic work of the anthropologist Claude Lévi-Strauss and the child psychologist Jean Piaget, the Structuralists see literature as "no more than a language, that is, a system of signs; its being lies not in the message but in the system. This being so, the critic is not called upon to reconstitute the *message* of the work, but only its *system*, just as the business of the linguist is not to decipher the *meaning* of a sentence but to determine the *formal structure* which permits the transmission of its meaning."[10]

Many poets active in the sixties were hostile not only to critics but to the very idea of literary criticism itself. Allen Ginsberg was vehement: "A word on Academies: poetry has been attacked by an ignorant and frightened bunch of bores who don't understand how it's made, & the trouble with these creeps is that they wouldn't know Poetry if it came up and buggered them in broad daylight."[11] Although John Berryman published many critical essays, he was not very interested in critical theory and commented, "When the mind dies, it exudes rich critical prose."[12] There are exceptions, of course, and poet-critics such as M. L. Rosenthal, Louis Simpson, A. Alvarez, Randall Jarrell, Richard Howard and Eric Mottram. Useful work on recent poetry has also been done by Marjorie Perloff, David Kalstone and others. What is absent is a criticism that affects poets writing now in the way that critical ideas affected the Romantic poets or the conventional poets of the fifties. The mood of the sixties was egalitarian, sometimes Marxist, often stressing "doing your own thing." Literary criticism was attacked as an elitist put-down whose value judgments reflected the monetary injustices of capitalist society. Anti-intellectualism prevailed, often citing the Dadaists as precedents and paralleled the Pop and Minimal movements in contemporary art. Susan Sontag's 1964 essay "Against Interpretation" was widely read: ". . . interpretation is the revenge of the intellect upon art. Even more. It is the revenge of the intellect upon the world. To interpret is to impoverish, to deplete the world— in order to set up a shadow world of 'meanings.' "[13]

Yet it is not so much literary criticism which some recent poets have suppressed but their awareness of why they write poems in certain ways and why they prefer some poems to others. Selection gave editors of magazines and presses guilt pangs in the sixties; sometimes guest editors and editorial committees were tried to give magazines as wide a scope as possible and to avoid the restrictive climate of the fifties. But even the most eclectic of editors did choose certain poems rather than others, and groups of poets coalesced, each with ideas and styles which became increasingly rigid boundaries against their avowed intentions of going beyond boundaries.

Predominant among the many concepts which recent poets have used to assess poetry is intensified awareness or expansion of consciousness. This means that a good poem does more than merely arouse an emotional thrill in its readers or satisfy the requirements of a certain form; it alters readers' perceptions of themselves and of reality. This change in perception may be delicate, as in a Japanese *haiku*, or the jolt may be dramatic, as in Allen Ginsberg's "Howl", but there is a definite shift in awareness. A poem's concentration of experience should act upon our perceptions as did Proust's magic lantern, which "substituted for the opaqueness of my walls an impalpable iridescence, supernatural phenomena of many colours, in which legends were depicted, as on a shifting and transitory window." [14] A powerful poem is a catalyst, taking us out of ourselves and into the intense moment that originally moved the poet.

Recent poets have made intensified awareness their goal. Charles Olson's manifesto "Projective Verse," first published in 1950, urged: ". . . always one perception must must must MOVE, INSTANTER, ON ANOTHER!" [15] Allen Ginsberg describes how he wrote "Howl":

"So the poem got serious, I went on to what my imagination believed true to Eternity (for I'd had a beatific illumination years before during which I'd heard Blake's ancient voice & saw the universe unfold in my brain), & what my memory could reconstitute of the data of celestial experience."[16] Denise Levertov ends her cogent essay "Some Notes on Organic Form" by referring to the "great gaps between perception and experience which must be leapt across if they are to be crossed at all. The X factor, the magic, is when we come to those rifts and make those leaps. A religious devotion to the truth, to the splendor of the authentic, involves the writer in a process rewarding in itself; but when that devotion brings us to undreamed abysses and we find ourselves sailing slowly over them and landing on the other side—that's ecstasy."[17] Lenore Kandel asserts: "Poetry is never compromise. It is the manifestation / translation of a vision, an illumination, an experience. If you compromise your vision you become a blind prophet."[18]

Although contemporary, this ideal of poetry as a means of intensifying awareness is not new and reflects the thinking of the French Symbolists, to a certain extent the Romantic poets, and the eighteenth-century philosophers who were influenced by the 1674 French translation of Longinus' *On the Sublime*. Longinus, a first-century Hellenist, based his literary judgments on the effect a poem had on its public, on the fact that it is "our nature to be elevated and exalted by true sublimity. Filled with joy and pride, we come to believe we have created what we have only heard."[19] E. F. N. Jephcott, in his extensive and illuminating book *Proust and Rilke: The Literature of Expanded Consciousness*, has shown how much understanding can be gained by exploring writers' struggle to convey their moments of extraordinary insight.

Let us use intensified awareness as our criterion to meet recent poets on their own terms, to be literally sympathetic with them. Our identification with these poets' outlook will eliminate some obscurity from their work. There are other ideas which have also affected contemporary poetry, but intensified awareness was many poets' goal and is a useful touchstone as we explore the many ways in which they tried to reach it.

As we look at each group of poets, I will begin each chapter with a matrix of ideas common to all of them, which the reader can then use as compass points to chart the directions taken not only by the poets discussed but also by similar poets. Of course the ideas shared by certain poets and categories for poets must be used for orientation only, and not imposed so clumsily that they blur the individual stamp of each poet (which is itself one thing we seek in good poetry).

This book is not a comprehensive roll-call of everyone writing poetry today. The poets chosen are the best, and the best representatives of the ideas in their groups, for these groups are more than a convenient way of looking at poets. The concepts these poets share not only aid our understanding of their poetry, but affected their writing of it. Although some poets resent being placed in a group, they still have styles and concerns in common with colleagues and often publish and are published by people who do similar work which they know and like. Some anthologists have rejected groupings as a distraction from the poems themselves and an incitement to carry on poetic feuds. However, clearly identifying the coteries of poets is also one way of exposing their deficiencies and ending the isolation that breeds their limitations.

Another question arises with respect to American and British poets: do they still have enough of a mutual language and tradition so that we may discuss them together, or are their environments and dictions so different that we must treat them as if they were writing in separate languages? Where there are important similarities we will consider American and British poets together, as in the chapter on conventional poets of the fifties and in the final chapter on newer poets. The differences of outlook between American and British poets and the recent movements in British poetry will be discussed in Chapter Eight, which is entirely on British poets.

Many of the innovations in contemporary poetry are reactions against previous conventions. In order to understand the forces that began to shape poetry after 1950 and the movements which have become well known since then, let us first look at the poets and critics who formed a powerful establishment during the fifties.

2

Still Life
from a Middle Distance:
Conventional Poets
of the Fifties

After Eliot's and Pound's startling experiments, after the apocalyptic poems of World War II, in the fifties many poets seemed to step aside and write from a placid detachment in conventional forms on non-controversial subjects. The fifties poets' middle distance was the emotional equivalent of a small college campus: a compromise between wilderness and the asphalt of a city center. Many poets' detachment was not expressed in far-out fantasy, but in a dispassionate, yet meticulous, photographing of reality.

One cause of this detachment was the exceptionally heavy influence of the New Criticism, which dominated the universities and literary journals at that time. This takeover was gradual and began as early as 1937, when Ransom's essay "Criticism Inc." was first published. William K. Wimsatt and M. C. Beardsley's essays "The Affective Fallacy" and "The Intentional Fallacy" followed in 1946 and 1949. By the early fifties New Critics were well entrenched in American colleges and universities such as Vanderbilt, Kenyon, Chicago and Yale. Through their students and numerous publications, the power of the New Critics persisted well into the sixties in many places.

New Criticism started partly as a reaction against the prevalent historical scholarship and intended that criticism should be absolutely objective. "Judging a poem is like judging a pudding or a machine," pronounced Wimsatt and Beardsley.[1] The New Critics' concept of "objectivity" went beyond fairness and disregard of prejudice in an attempt to make criticism as precise and logical as science. These university teachers found it advantageous to regard criticism as a science, for that meant it was a subject which could be taught. Critics were to be made by training intellects, rather than by cultivating those with natural talents. Ransom sounded like a businessman worried about competition and calling for trade restrictions when he said: "Rather than occasional criticism by amateurs, I should think the whole enterprise might be seriously taken in hand by professionals."[2] Ransom's commercial tone was quite deliberate, and he emphasized it by the title "Criticism Inc." This business ethos was to have a wide appeal in the fifties: what was good for General Motors was not only good for America but good for poetry. Criticism as a science, as a business, was a concept that could be grasped by university administrators and boards of trustees who decided on teachers' tenure.

The New Critics had a particular horror of personal views and of emotional reactions, both by critics and by poets. The "Affective Fallacy," judging a poem by its effect on its readers, was scrupulously denounced as heresy by Wimsatt and Beardsley. However, objectivity proved to be an unobtainable ideal, and an examination of the criticism actually written in the fifties shows it to be as bedeviled by feuds and even-handed stabs in the back as that of any other era. The New Critics' detailed analysis of safely dead poets avoided the risks of adventurous choices or courageous conclusions.

The worst failing of New Criticism was that it was not flexible in response to the good poets of its day and actually inhibited younger poets, forcing them to adopt extreme positions in reaction to it. Wimsatt and Beardsley in particular are envious and condescending toward working poets and their untidy emotions. New Critical ideas which were intended for the *assessing* of poetry were widely misunderstood to be guidelines for the *writing* of poetry. Academic poets working according to these formulas found a ready market for their verses as fillers in the columns of prestigious magazines.

The effects of New Criticism were not all negative. Some of the techniques and ideas adapted (but not necessarily invented) by the New Critics are useful in understanding poets of the fifties. The concept of the poet's *persona* provides a way into Philip Larkin's poems, and the concept of irony enriches our appreciation of D. J. Enright's work. Richard Wilbur's poems reward detailed analysis, and an under-standing of the need for distance and for dry wit increases our en-joyment of Howard Nemerov's poems. Out of the many poets who made their reputations about that time, I would like to concentrate on these four since they shared ideas common to other poets of that de-cade and they are still writing at present. Although such fine but de-ceased poets as Jarrell and Roethke must be excluded, these four living poets have progressed beyond the attitudes of the fifties and are significant today.

Philip Larkin earned a wide reputation from the mid-fifties onward, partly becaused he expressed the semi-detached mood of that era. In one of his best-known poems, "Whitsun Weddings," Larkin rides on a train to London, and at first he does not even glance up from his book to see what the commotion is at each station. When he does look through the window, the bystanders on the platforms are remote, "as if out on the end of an event".[3] Looking again, Larkin realizes that these are wedding parties waving goodby to newlyweds boarding the train. "The fathers with broad belts under their suits / And seamy foreheads; mothers loud and fat; / An uncle shouting smut; and then the perms, / The nylon gloves and jewellery-substitutes, / The lemons, mauves, and olive-ochres that / Marked off the girls unreally from the rest."[4] Another reason for Larkin's popularity is that his poems are not ob-scure; it is easy for the reader to trace the outlines of their subject mat-ter, which is usually ordinary people and their relationships. Some-times, as above, Larkin's view is accurate but condescending toward the lower middle classes; this tone appeals to certain members of the British intelligensia.

Larkin frequently portrays everyday reality as not only common but dismal. "Life is first boredom, then fear / Whether or not we use it, it goes."[5] No consolation is allowed from fantasies, history, hope for the future or foreign travel. Larkin vigorously rejected Roman-ticism and titled his second book of poems *The Less Deceived*. Es-capism's delusions may tempt him, as in "Toads," but he dispells them with harsh facts: "Ah, were I courageous enough / To shout *Stuff your pension!* / But I know, all too well, that's the stuff / That dreams are made on."[6] This depressive outlook absolves its holder from regretting past losses, trying to improve the present or risking any hope on the future. It is uncomfortable, but familiar, like the cheap bed in a furnished room.

But when Larkin repeats this drab attitude in a number of poems, readers may become discouraged. Here we must distinguish between the poem itself and the poet's *persona*, the social façade a poet projects to meet his audience. The apparently informal, conversational style of much recent poetry can mislead us into judging a poem as we would judge chat, and into accepting or rejecting the poet's *persona* as if it were the poet himself and we were deciding whether or not to invite him to dinner. Larkin intends his *persona* to be totally frank if unflattering. He has spoken of his "sense of relief that I didn't have to try and jack myself up to a concept of poetry that lay outside my own life . . . One could simply relapse back into one's own life and write about it."[7]

The familiar, then, is both Larkin's subject and his strength. For without being mystical, he sees the everyday take on an added dimension, just as the prize vegetables in "Show Saturday" acquire a glow because they are the "single, supreme visions" of ordinary people.[8] When his poems are not completely successful it is because their transmission of the depths and nuances of their ordinary subjects is limited and untrue to Larkin's own understanding. He is aware of this inadequacy, and even in one of his glummest portraits, "Mr. Bleaney," Larkin doubts that he knows the man's innermost thoughts, although he knows his superficial habits.

This difficulty in comprehending his subjects arose partly from the skeptical attitude of fifties poets, who proclaimed in one manifesto that they were "bored by the despair of the forties, not much interested in suffering and extremely impatient of poetic sensibility."[9] One means by which Larkin outgrew this restricting mood was his lifelong interest in jazz, which is sensual, improvisatory, chromatic and intimate—all qualities opposed to the fifties ethos. (Jazz is also non-English, non-white.) In "For Sidney Bechet," Larkin deliberately rejects any fantasies about jazz and is thus able to welcome it as "the natural noise of good, / Scattering long-haired grief and scored pity."[10] Larkin's later poems have become more sensual in their images, as in this seascape: "Rocks writhe back to sight. / Mussels, limpets, / Husband their tenacity / In the freezing slither— / Creatures, I cherish you!"[11] When his affirmations of life come, they are strong and striking against his backdrop of unremitting realism: "What will survive of us is love."[12] For

Philip Larkin, the problems of love, death, human futility and loneliness were all tangled together, and he steadfastly refused to accept any separate or glib answers.

How does a conventional poet such as Larkin satisfy our criterion of intensifying the reader's awareness? He has said his aim in writing a poem is "to construct a verbal device that would preserve an experience indefinitely by reproducing it in whoever read the poem.[13] He so successfully distills the essence of certain realities that it is impossible to encounter them again without remembering Larkin's words. Many readers now find that every time they enter a branch of a certain British chain store they hear Larkin describing "The large cool store selling cheap clothes / Set out in simple sizes plainly. . . .[14]

One of Larkin's most admirable qualities is his discretion: although he only publishes one slim volume every ten years or so, almost every poem in his books is excellent (if not agreeable). He uses neat end rhymes in most of his poems (rather cautiously in the early ones), and there are faint echoes of Hopkins in the stressed long syllables. Some of his more recent poems are structured with insistent, exact imagery and condensed metaphors, such as "radio rubs its legs."[15] This change in style reflects the change in poetic atmosphere from the sixties onward, which also affected conventional poets such as Larkin. Larkin is one of those poets whose work improves with maturity; in 1980 he was fifty-eight years old, an age at which Yeats (whose influence can be seen in Larkin's first book) was writing some of his strongest poems. Hardy, Larkin's favorite poet, produced some of his best work in his seventies. Now that Larkin has transcended the emotional limitations of the fifties we can confidently expect more integrated and exciting poems from him in the next decade.

For a large part of his life D. J. Enright has put an actual distance between himself and the England of his birth by teaching in universities in Bangkok, Singapore, Alexandria and Kobe. Yet in his poems these exotic settings define by contrast his English attitudes and views of his country. Enright is well aware of the tricks memory and imagination can play, and one of his poems portrays an Egyptian who longs for Alexandria and is miserable in Birmingham: "surely the world's burst conscience overhangs this island."[16] But Enright's Egyptian is also astute enough to realize that eventually he will become bored back in Alexandria and entertain his cronies with tales of fabulous Birmingham, whose fame will "ripple through the bazaars like a belly dancer— / A city of peril, like the shark, a city of witty Gohas, / Your streets astream with passions, big as buses, / Brown jinn shall squat upon your chimneys, ravage the countryside— / Your chanting pigeons, at evening, be princesses and enchanted." [17] Unlike Larkin, Enright allows the workaday present to be transformed by imagination, memory and hope, even if he is aware of their distortions.

Words, too, can be inadequate to the wonder of actual things, and Enright says the purpose of writing poetry may be "To prove the dishonesty of names and their black greed— / To confess your ignorance, to expiate your crime, / seeking a spell to lift a curse." [18] This poem, "Blue Umbrellas," was prompted by a child who asked the name of "the thing that makes a blue umbrella with its tail" and Enright's dissatisfaction with his answer, "peacock." Enright combats the weakness of words by deft contrasts of light and dark, quicksilver changes from comic to serious. "Only extremes should meet / Without contraries there is no progress." [19] One way he accomplishes this is by a highly skilled use of puns, such as his father "dying in error / Eire." [20]

Perhaps Enright's best book is *The Terrible Shears*, a long sequence of poems about his impoverished childhood. He is able to write about even the most poignant events of growing up with unblinking honesty, reticence and wit that banish sentimentality. Once he and his sister discovered a musical box, hidden away to be a present for their new baby sister. "Just before Christmas (this I know is a memory / For no one ever spoke of it) the baby quietly / Disgorged a lot of blood, and was taken away. / The musical box disappeared too, / As my sister and I noted with mixed feelings. / We were not too old to play with it." [21] We readers are also left "with mixed feelings" after many of Enright's poems, for our expectations have been dexterously reversed, our prejudices shrewdly overturned. Enright's essential talent is an openness to emotional involvement combined with a witty perspective that together yield an insight beyond himself and beyond any brief occasion.

Enright is a humanist, in the best sense of the word, concerned with people and acutely aware of the political injustices which he not only saw in the Middle and Far East, but on several occasions suffered. (One night in Bangkok he and his wife were beaten up by drunken policemen; the British consul's response was to apologize to the police.) Yet although Enright's sense of right and wrong is keen, he doesn't preach doctrinal political solutions. In "Hands Off, Foreign Devil," he listens as his Chinese typist tells him her problems and watches as she crushes ants on her desk: "I turn toward the window, / Listening to her, but not looking, / Not lecturing. The country's hers, / Not mine. The ants, too, I suppose."[22]

In many of his recent poems, Enright has almost completely moved away from rhyme and instead welds his poems together with concepts. He publishes a large number of poems (in addition to criticism and fiction); his tone is conversational, even prosy, and sometimes a bit slack. But at his best, he combines the opposites of engagement with reality and witty distance to wake us up as does "The Noodle-Vendor's Flute" in the Japanese night:

> The flute itself a counterfeit
> (Siberian wind can freeze the lips),
> Merely a rubber bulb and metal horn
> (Hard to ride a cycle, watch for manholes
> And late drunks, and play a flute together).
> Just squeeze between gloved fingers,
> And the note of mild hope sounds:
> Release, the indrawn sigh of mild despair. . . .
> And I, like other listeners,
> See my stupid sadness as a common thing.
> And being common,
> Therefore something rare indeed.
> The puffing vendor, surer than a trumpet,
> Tells us we are not alone.
> Each night that same frail midnight tune
> Squeezed from a bogus flute,
> Under the noise of war, after war's noise,
> It mourns the fallen, every night,
> It celebrates survival—
> In real cities, real houses, real time.[23]

Enright's distance, his Japanese mock flute, ultimately return him and us to the things that are very real indeed.

One dominant figure in American poetry since the early fifties has been Richard Wilbur, who has collected many laurels from universities and almost as many brickbats from attackers of "academic" poetry. He has been influential, not only by the example of his style, but through his many French translations, his teaching posts, his critical writings and his editing of a series of new poetry published by Wesleyan University Press (a sure-fire way to earn the loathing of any younger poet whose manuscript was rejected!). Adept at many formal constructions of verse, he often writes in rhyme or even in intricate Provençal forms such as the villanelle. Richard Wilbur's main strength is his skill, a dedicated craftsmanship that has persisted over the years. His attitude is the opposte of that of the makers of shoddy goods which he describes in "Junk." The poem's epigraph, taken from a fragmentary Anglo-Saxon poem, concerns the legendary smith Wayland, and may roughly be translated: "Truly, Wayland's handiwork—the sword Mimming which he made—will never fail any man who knows how to use it bravely."

An axe angles
                    from my neighbor's ashcan:
It is hell's handiwork,
                    the wood not hickory,
The flow of the grain
                    not faithfully followed.
The shivered shaft
                    rises from a shellheap
Of plastic playthings,
                    paper plates,
And the sheer shards
                    of shattered tumblers
That were not annealed
                    for the time needful.
At the same curbside,
                    a cast-off cabinet
Of wavily-warped
                    unseasoned wood
Waits to be trundled
                    in the trash-man's truck.
Haul them off! Hide them!
                    The heart winces
For junk and gimcrack,
                    for jerrybuilt things

And the men who make them
                              for a little money,
Bartering pride
                    like the bought boxer
Who pulls his punches,
                              or the paid-off jockey
Who in the home stretch
                              holds in his horse.
Yet the things themselves
                              in thoughtless honor
Have kept composure,
                              like captives who would not
Talk under torture.
                       Tossed from a tailgate
Where the dump displays
                              its random dolmens,
Its black barrows
                    and blazing valleys,
They shall waste in the weather
                                   toward what they were.
The sun shall glory
                       in the glitter of glass-chips,
Foreseeing the salvage
                          of the prisoned sand,
And the blistering paint
                          peel off in patches,
That the good grain
                       be discovered again.
Then burnt, bulldozed,
                          they shall all be buried
To the depth of diamonds,
                             in the making dark
Where halt Hephaestus
                          keeps his hammer
And Wayland's work
                       is worn away. [24]

Wilbur adapts with ease the Anglo-Saxon device of alliteration to
connect the lines and half-lines. He does not slavishly follow the

Anglo-Saxon model, however, and wisely does not impose its strict meters or its *kennings*, complex metaphors. His use of this dense form is no mere exercise in style, but an expression of the complexities underlying common tools and the danger when they are badly made. Since Richard Wilbur was raised on a farm in New Jersey, we may suppose that he was taught from an early age always to check that an axe head is tight and its shaft uncracked before chopping with it. For a loose axe head can careen through the air, maim and even kill. The "shell heap / of plastic playthings" may not be as physically menacing as the axe or broken glass but is emotionally wounding to small children: new toys that break as soon as anyone plays with them, whose thin sharp plastic cannot be glued together. The cabinet's warped wood probably causes its drawers to stick, an almost unconscious but daily annoyance. "Annealed" in line seven is an unusual word, but exactly right, for it means to toughen after fusion by continuous and slowly diminishing heat. It is derived from the Old English *onǣlan*, "to set on fire," and is akin to the Old English word for funeral pyre. Richard Wilbur, with a translator's patience, searches for the precise word both to convey his immediate meaning and to reverberate with deeper connotations. (This is also typical of Marianne Moore's work, which was an early influence on Wilbur.)

Like many of Wilbur's poems, "Junk" examines the details of objects, such as the flow of the grain in the axe handle and the paint blisters. This incisive and relentless fine focus can reveal the unexpected: "a glitter of glass chips," "the depth of diamonds." However, too many small-scale poems (particularly by Wilbur's weaker imitators) can be enervating and cramping when read together. Paradoxically, although their detail is finely drawn, the objects themselves are abstract: the junk-heap is nowhere in particular; the wood of the splintered axe-handle is merely "not hickory"; the playthings are not specified; and the peeling paint has no color. Readers can use their imagination to color in these objects from their own experiences, thus giving the poem meaning on a wider scale. In "Junk" the objects are melting in the dump fire and weathering toward their basic elements. Problems with this technique can occur when objects that are intended to have a general meaning appear so bland that they have no personal immediacy, like letters addressed to "Occupant." A poem such as "The Agent" fails to convince us, although it is carefully written, because the country, the conflict and the spy are too anonymous; he is a man "who cannot name the streets of his own town."[25]

Richard Wilbur does not attempt the All-American Epic Poem, nor is he outspokenly American, or concerned to record and evolve a distinctively native twang. When he does use a word with a strongly American flavor, such as "gimcrack" in "Junk", it slides naturally into place and is not a self-conscious straining after dialect. He has sometimes been indicted for a lack of passion and disinterest in social issues. A close reading of all his poems shows this is not entirely justified: "The Pardon" and "Advice to a Prophet" are keenly felt and show a wide concern. There is a deliberate distance between blunt emotion and the finished poem, but it is the distance of craft, not callousness. Wilbur's gifts are more of the eye's insight than the ear's easy music. Although every line is well tuned, we sense a great struggle has gone on backstage, and some of the end rhymes land with heavy clumps.

The frequent references to mythology in Wilbur's work are typical of American academic poetry of the fifties. When these references are well integrated, they add resonance and scope to his poems, as is the case with "Junk." Hephaestus, son of Zeus and Hera, was born lame and became smith to the gods, making many magical weapons for them. He lived under the volcano of Mt. Etna, and Aphrodite was his unfaithful wife. With an axe Hephaestus split apart Zeus' skull so Athena could be born. In Anglo-Saxon mythology, Wayland the Smith's magical sword Mimming was captured from him together with other treasure by King Niduth, who ordered the smith to be lamed and imprisoned. But Wayland's skill enabled him to take a horrible revenge: he lured the king's two sons into his cell with a promise of a chest of gold and jewels, then slammed the lid on their necks, murdering them. Their skulls he embellished with silver and sent to the king, who unwittingly used them for drinking cups; their eyes Wayland transformed into jewels which the queen wore; their teeth became breast ornaments for their sister. Wayland's artifacts were "hell's handiwork"—ingenious but gruesome. Wayland raped the king's daughter after giving her a sleeping potion, left her pregnant and escaped on wings which he fashioned from bird feathers.[26] How much of this mythic material can the average reader by expected to know? Hephaestus probably, and Wayland is footnoted. Neither reference is vital to a superficial comprehension of the poem, although both can be looked up easily and the search adds dimensions. Used clumsily, mythological references can slow or even stop the reader who is not familiar with them or persistent enough to ferret out obscure points. Myth often becomes a distancing device for handling themes that are too personal to be dealt with directly.

One of the most admirable traits of conventional fifties poets is exemplified by Richard Wilbur's untiring workmanship and his refusal to be content with gimcrack. While his poems do not go off limits with new forms, explosive subjects or forbidden passions, their high concentration of images causes the reader's vision of reality to implode into a new world as wide and surprising as a first look through a microscope.

How refreshing Howard Nemerov's jokes are, after the pomposity of so many fifties poets. Nemerov has said that certain kinds of poems are a way of getting things right in language in the same way that a joke is a way of getting things right in language. Not only is his characteristic dry wit amusing, it is "wit" in the sense derived from the root word for knowledge. While Wilbur's lines pace steadily toward their conclusions, where rhymes frequently cap them, a line by Nemerov often swivels and pivots on a witticism that suddenly pins our attention on a comic anomaly. As he walks along the rows of plants in a nursery, he reads "their Latin names, / their American prices."[27] Although Nemerov is usually pigeonholed among the academics, he has an acute ear for the speech of ordinary people, as in "The Beekeeper Speaks" or his portrait of the Biblical Lot as a harassed Jewish businessman who pleads with God for a quiet retirement: " 'A small house will do. / Only I shouldn't be part of history.' Of course no one answered."[28] Wit may be a quiet fulcrum within a serious poem or the force behind a full-scale satire such as "A Full Professor": "Publish or perish! What frightful chance! / It troubled him through all his early days. / But now he has the system beat both ways: / He publishes and perishes at once."[29]

There is a self-mocking tone in this poem and a cheeky illiteracy—"has the system beat." And as in so many of Nemerov's humorous poems, there is an underlying sadness that carries the poem beyond mere light verse and leaves us uneasy, as if the poem were a wrinkled copy of *The New Yorker* or *Punch* that does not quite divert us in the dentist's waiting room from our imminent appointment. Sometimes this discomfort becomes the full primitive terrors of childhood, as when Nemerov watches with his son sadistic cartoons on TV, or remembers the blind maid shaking a stick on a can of Dutch Cleanser in his early nightmares or the menace in an ordinary vacuum cleaner:

> The house is so quiet now
> The vacuum cleaner sulks in the corner closet,
> Its bag limp as a stopped lung, its mouth
> Grinning into the floor, maybe at my
> Slovenly life, my dog-dead youth.
>
> I've lived this way long enough,
> But when my old woman died her soul
> Went into that vacuum cleaner, and I can't bear
> To see the bag swell like a belly, eating the dust
> And the woolen mice, and begin to howl
>
> Because there is old filth everywhere
> She used to crawl, in the corner and under the stair.
> I know now how life is cheap as dirt,
> And still the hungry, angry heart
> Hangs on and howls, biting at air.[30]

"Woolen mice" is an apt and inventive term for those gray lumps of dust that flit under beds, and it echoes the helplessness the poet may have felt as a child threatened by emotional vacuums.

As witty as Nemerov's funniest poems are, we must not be misled by them, or by the terse poker-playing *persona* which he sometimes adopts, into dismissing him as a light entertainer. (He may be the only poet who has mentioned such a mundane worry as the mortgage on his house and gotten away with it.) The world of nature almost immediately prompts him to speculate about metaphysical questions, such as the problems of time and being raised by a running stream's simultaneous motion and stasis. Nemerov's eagerness to hurry beyond the surface of things can give the plants and animals in some of his nature poems a flat, unremarkable presence. He assumes his reader is interested in philosophical problems and, while Nemerov is willing to be convivial, he refuses to water down complexities. There are some mythological references too, although they are not as dense as in Wilbur's work.

Nemerov's style is streamlined; its skillfully timed jokes and revelations are unencumbered by verbal padding. This trim style is neither radically new nor obviously derivative (except for some echoes of Yeats in early poems). It is an instrument, rather than an end in itself, and it is finely honed to do exactly what the poet intends. A reader willing to probe beneath the polished surface of Nemerov's style will not only encounter witty incongruities and reversals, but will hear the quieter echoes inherent in Nemerov's living subjects.

While these four poets are representative of the tone of conventional fifties poetry, they do not entirely convey the rigid orthodoxy which prevailed at that time. The "New" Critics in America and the "Movement" in England actually enforced the "old" and the "stable." Not only was innovation unwelcome, but any extension of poetry's bounds was taboo. Robert Conquest, introducing an anthology of his fellow "Movement" poets such as Kingsley Amis, Anthony Thwaite, Elizabeth Jennings, Donald Davie, Philip Larkin, John Wain and D. J. Enright, said: "The tendency in the last forty or fifty years has been not merely to grossly exaggerate the importance of poets who have in some sort extended the range of the art, but actually to imply that any such extension, or even attempt at extension, is itself a sign of quality."[31] (As we shall see, expansion of poetry's range has indeed become the aim of most recent poets.) All too often the fifties' unadventurous attitudes produced bland, buttoned-down verses with predictable comparisons and obvious conclusions.

Yet the fifties' rigorous standards also meant that the best poets paid attention to craft, buffed their language to a high gloss and were careful about what they published. As well as Philip Larkin staring silently out of a train window, the stance of these conventional poets included the skill and detachment that give Howard Nemerov a firm hold on real life as he stands on a bridge above the blue swallows which fly between it and the stream:

> Across the millstream below the bridge
> Seven blue swallows divide the air
> In shapes invisible and evanescent,
> Kaleidoscopic beyond the mind's
> Or memory's power to keep them there. . . .

O swallows, swallows, poems are not
The point. Finding again the world,
That is the point, where loveliness
Adorns intelligible things
Because the mind's eye lit the sun.[32]

3

"The Will to Change":
The Black Mountain Poets

Almost every campus has one: a teacher whose lectures are crowded and controversial, who has disciples and despisers, who is simultaneously an anarchist and a high priest. As his students grow older, they will probably realize that many of his dazzling flashes of insight were secondhand hokum, yet he will always remain the teacher they remember most vividly. For it was not what he actually said that set his students alight, but his energetic and irreverent way of saying it, which was attuned to their own youthful zest and iconoclasm. Charles Olson was such a teacher, not only for his own college but for an entire generation of American poets. Some poets, such as Ed Dorn and Jonathan Williams, were Olson's students; others, such as Robert Duncan and Denise Levertov, were his friends and correspondents. Hence the term "Black Mountain poets" is not limited to the small progressive college in North Carolina where Olson taught, or to *Black Mountain Review*, which published many of these poets' early work, but also encompasses a wider group of poets who were influenced by Olson's theory of Projective Verse as well as by him personally. Black Mountain poetry works in spite of its theory; yet without this theory, the poetry wouldn't have been possible. Olson's personality was needed as a counterweight to Eliot and other big-name poets of the early fifties, and his Projective Verse theory was also needed as an alternative to the all-pervasive New Criticism.

Each group of new poets uses various tactics to come to terms with the work of the poets who immediately precede them. Some poets deny the value of all work by their predecessors and react against them by writing in contrary styles. (This is particularly appealing to poets in America, where so much value is placed on anything "new.") Other poets will cite the ideas of much older poets and reject their immediate predecessors. Still others will accept their elders' influence but will deliberately misunderstand this older work in order to make space for new poems. Harold Bloom has called this relation "the anxiety of influence" and modeled his theory on the Freudian Oedipal conflict between children and parents. "Weaker talents idealize; figures of capable imagination appropriate for themselves. But nothing is got for nothing, and self-appropriation involves the immense anxieties of indebtedness, for what strong maker desires the realization that he has failed to create himself?" [1] When the Black Mountain group began to form their ideas about poetry in the early fifties they were heavily influenced by Pound and William Carlos Williams, but they found these influences so unacceptable that they had to use Olson as an intermediary and claimed that they were following Olson's "new" theory of Projective Verse rather than Pound and Williams.

The anxiety that Pound generated in poets coming after him is understandable, and has a number of causes. First, Pound wrote *The Cantos*, a vast, ambitious work of daunting erudition, whose best sections have been widely acclaimed as among the finest poetry written in this century. But Pound's life and beliefs are repugnant to many poets; in the later Cantos his powers had clearly degenerated; he was charged with treason after making a number of pro-Axis broadcasts from Mussolini's Italy. Found unfit to plead because of insanity, he was committed to St. Elizabeth's Hospital in Washington, D.C., for eleven years. Despite the apology often given that Pound was insane when he so openly advocated totalitarianism, he had given public vent to his fascism and crude anti-Semitism for many years beforehand. Poets following Pound are presented with a dilemma: either a poet's work is completely separate from his life and his political views; or, if a poet's writing is an indivisible part of his life, then any repulsive acts in his life must be excused as a result of the madness which poets necessarily risk. Pound is a problem especially for many poets who had strong left-wing views in the sixties: was it logical to picket the Pentagon with placards calling Lyndon Johnson a fascist yet at the same time laud

Ezra Pound's poetry and theories and imitate his style? But Olson's theory of Projective Verse had had the madness and fascism filtered out of it.

Also, Pound had been living in Europe for most of his life, drawing his inspiration from sophisticated sources such as Calvalcanti, Dante, ancient Chinese poets, Homer and Villon, while the younger poets were concerned to find an authentic American idiom, a new language for a New World, and to continue the tradition of Walt Whitman. Olson was their man: not only did he return to the small town where he had grown up (something few poets have the nerve to do), but he eulogized it in his epic *Maximus* poems.

Why then, if mythologizing the ordinary Americana of a small town was the ideal of younger poets, couldn't they accept the critical ideas of Williams without the intermediary of Olson's theory of Projective Verse? Williams was *too* domestic, provincial, familiar—in short, *too* American in the Age of Eisenhower, when many poets felt they had to proclaim their dissent from the exclusively American Dream or be suffocated by it. Olson's Gloucester, Massachusetts, was perched on the edge of America; indeed the map Olson chose for the cover of *Maximus IV, V, VI* shows the American, European and African continents still touching 125 million years ago before they broke apart to form the Atlantic Ocean. The *Maximus* poems abound in references to early English colonists and Greek mythology. When Olson explored the past, he chose the exotic but indisputably American past; he worked seriously as an archaeologist on a dig in Yucatan and found the Mayan culture an inspiration.

Three major aspects of Pound's and Williams's work influenced Olson's theory of Projective Verse. First, the concept of simultaneous history dispensed with time barriers as artificial. In Pound's *The Cantos*, especially, many past and present events appear at the same moment like a crowd of ghosts at a séance. Second, just as history was seen as simultaneous events rather than a temporal sequence, so Olson considered the poem to be a "field" full of simultaneous words, images and sounds, rather than a linear sequence. He declared that a poet must venture into the open, away from previous forms of stanzas, lines, etc., and let the poem decide its own form. Third, in practical terms, "composition by field" was reflected in experiments in typography which used the typewriter's spacing and punctuation marks in unconventional ways, as if the page were a painter's canvas. Pound's and

Williams's typography and spelling, experimental in their day, became mannerisms for the Black Mountain School, whose poems sometimes looked like telegrams sent home by impoverished, illiterate college students asking for money: omission of the *e* in the ending *-ed*; all letters lower case; and random phonic spellings such as *enuf, thot, nite, delite,* etc.

Although Olson sometimes nodded politely toward Pound's and Williams's work, when he was confronted directly with his indebtedness he was enraged: "I just damn well don't like the establishing of *relations*. They are phoneys."[2] Yet in Olson's own poetry, he frequently attempts to draw relations between diverse and far-ranging subjects. In a letter to Robert Creeley, Olson explained why he discounted Pound and Williams: ". . . another reason why i don't think Ez's toucan works after 1917 is, that, after that date, the materials of history which he has found useful are not at all of use (nor are Bill's, despite the more apparent homogeneity: date 1917, not only did Yurrup (West, Cento, Renaissance) go, but such blueberry America as Bill presents (Jersey dump-smoke covering same) also WENT (that is, Bill, with all respect, don't know fr nothing abt what a city *is*)."[3]

Stated in its simplest form, Olson's Projective Verse theory has three main principles. The first is that a poem must be a high "energy discharge" from the poet to the reader. Second, the form of a poem is an extension of its content. And third, "ONE PERCEPTION MUST IMMEDIATELY AND DIRECTLY LEAD TO A FURTHER PERCEPTION."[4] Olson's essay "Projective Verse" originally appeared in 1950; by 1960 the Projective Verse theory was widely acclaimed as the dominant new concept, and it had great prestige through the sixties and seventies. However, many objections to Projective Verse have been raised. Certainly it was not as new as its supporters claimed, but a patchwork of Pound's and Williams's ideas, as has been convincingly demonstrated by Marjorie Perloff.[5] The trouble with this theory is that it remained a manifesto, rather than a progenitor of engaged, practical criticism that aided the actual writing of poetry. Projective Verse's effect, despite its wide popularity, was *introspective*, the breath of each poet being the sole criterion for the length and meter of his poetry, rather than *projective*, the effect on readers determining the form of the poem. Olson himself, when he wanted to criticize others' poems, was surprisingly inarticulate, despite his fervor: "I am so sick of this sort of thing you show me from Bronk-the green of it, the green-sick, too—the bad-headedness, as well as the manners. . . ."[6] Olson never tells Cid Corman (editor of *Origin*, which first published many Black Mountain poets) exactly what he likes or dislikes about these poems, much less uses his Projective Verse theory as a critical instrument. Nor were the poets whom Olson influenced able to use the theory to discuss coherently their own and others' poems.

The most crucial question we must ask about the Projective Verse theory is, did it help Olson to write his own poetry? As he himself says, "So there we are, fast, there's the dogma. And its excuse, its usableness in practice."[7] "Projective Verse" was written before Olson wrote the bulk of his poetry. The first principle Olson states is "the *kinetics* of the thing. A poem is energy transferred from where the poet got it (he will have several causations), by way of the poem itself to, all the way over to, the reader. Okay. Then the poem itself must, at all points, be a high energy-construct and, at all points, an energy-discharge."[8] But energy is what is so conspicuously lacking from Olson's major work, the voluminous *Maximus* poems. Here the "field of the poem" frequently becomes a Massachusetts cranberry bog: a morass of quaint olde ships' logs, provincial topography, miscellaneous mythology, inventories and unimaginative trivia into which the reader's attention soon sinks without a ripple.

This composition method of Olson's reflects his second principle: "FORM IS NEVER MORE THAN AN EXTENSION OF CONTENT." Although Olson cites Robert Creeley as his source, this idea is a reversion to the ancient Aristotelian concept that the form of a work of art should imitate its subject. Olson takes it to the extreme of saying that in a poem "the line comes (I swear it) from the breath, from the breathing of the man who writes, at the moment that he writes, and thus is, it is here that, the daily work, the WORK, gets in, for only he, the man who writes, can declare, at every moment, the line its metric and its ending—where its breathing, shall come to, termination."[9] The man who writes becomes the content of his poem: "For man is himself an object" related to nature but "breath is man's special qualification as an animal. Sound is a dimension he has extended. Language is one of his proudest acts."[10] If the line endings in Olson's poems are meant to indicate breath stops, then the breathing is often arbitrary and asthmatic.

Olson's third principle of Projective Verse is: "ONE PERCEPTION
MUST IMMEDIATELY AND DIRECTLY LEAD TO A FURTHER PERCEPTION."
But Olson will often repeat the same perception in his own poetry.
For example, a 1956 poem, "The Lordly and Isolate Satyrs," begins
engagingly. The calm of a beach is disturbed when satyrs/boddisat-
vahs/a motorcycle club ride in and halt between the viewers/poet and
the sea: "—we did not notice them until they were already creating /
the beach we had not known was there—. . . ."[11] This is an exciting
perception but, instead of leading on to other perceptions, Olson
repeats it four more times. The same image of the satyrs is repeated in
line 86, "boddisatvah" recurs in line 73 and 105, Easter Island is invoked in line 12 and again in line 65 and echoed in the "Great /
Stones" of lines 31–32. Other needless repetitions mar Olson's vision
of the bikers metamorphosing into satyrs, boddisatvahs (Sanskrit: "one
enlightened in essence"), and freckled adolescents, then back into
transforming demi-gods. Despite its interesting moments, this verbose,
repetitive poem is certainly not an example of Olson's exhortation that
"in any given poem always, always one perception must must must
MOVE, INSTANTER, ON ANOTHER!"[12]

Olson's attempts to eliminate a time sequence often result in
poems that lack a dramatic climax. Even in the final book of *Maximus*
poems, when Olson's lyric gifts are most powerful, the climactic
images have been rented for the occasion. "This / is the rose is the
rose of the World."[13] This image is anticlimactic not only because its
phrasing neatly echoes Gertrude Stein, but because it has been used so
many times before, most notably by Dante in Cantos XXX and XXXI
of *Paradiso,* where the souls of the blessed form the flaming petals of a
white rose. But unlike Dante, Olson has no consistent philosophical
structure undergirding his epic. Dante's world view was a highly sys-
tematized Christian one, accessible to his readers. Pound's early and
middle *Cantos* rested on a westernized Confucianism. Williams's *Pa-
terson* intensified to the level of universal myth a single locality and its
people. Olson also attempts to do this with his Gloucester, Massachusetts, but his mythologizing is too self-conscious and not coherently integrated.

Olson's view of the poem as energy transferred from the poet to the
reader is somewhat similar to the criterion we have adopted, that a
good poem intensifies the reader's awareness. Certainly there are some
striking lyric moments in *Maximus:*

the mists of the Indians
on the land, the flow,
from the ice, of the hidden
speech, the tales they tell
of the m'teoulin, of the masques performed
in the waves, of the Indian watchers making on
to these other men who have come to the shore
the fogs the fogs are especially noted you can walk at night
and read your shadow slanted upward by your side, the tales
the tales to tell in the continuous speech.[14]

These passages break through the dead weight of Projective Verse theory, the mannerisms borrowed from Williams and the strictures of Pound's style. Olson's individuality became increasingly powerful toward the last *Maximus* poems, written the year before his death in 1970 at the relatively early age of sixty. If he had been given more time to escape the influence of Pound and Williams, and had accepted more practical criticism from his peers, then Olson's own gifts might have come to more fruition. "I can only cry: Those / who gave you not enough / caused you to settle for / too little."[15]

Olson's most valuable contribution to contemporary poetry was not his own poems, or even his ramshackle theory of Projective Verse, but his gusto and contagious love of poetry. Never, never must we underestimate the absolute necessity of enthusiasm and interchange between poets if poetry is to remain alive. Writing poetry is a lonely, difficult and unappreciated task; publishing a little magazine or a poetry press can be even more discouraging and harder on the pocket. Olson helped to create an open climate in which poetry of a certain sort could be written by anyone, whatever their natural gifts, persistence or learning. (This free-for-all did not mean, however, that everyone wrote good poems—only that more people tried.) Some of Olson's gift for friendship and his impact on other poets is evident in his published correspondence. Once, when he was furious at the comparison of his poems to Pound's and Williams's work, Olson fired off a scatological letter to Cid Corman. Corman replied mildly and Olson, in his turn, apologized: "i'm a hot one. And you sure cooled me . . . with no rebuke for, me jumping all over, you, and you only saying wot was yr thot i just have to demand of you, special, simply, that you have been so much my friend"[16] Olson did demand much of his poet friends:

and his special demands made him both exasperating and energizing
to the Black Mountain movement.

Robert Creeley was a close friend of Charles Olson's, edited *Black
Mountain Review* and taught at the college, but Creeley's poems are
quite different from Olson's work. Creeley writes on a personal scale:
human relationships provide the main content of his poems. "Nothing
grand— / The scale is neither / big nor small."[17] Rhapsodic love
poems are frequent in his early work, traditional in their attitude if not
their form. "The love of a woman / is the possibility which / surrounds
her as hair / her head, as the love of her / follows and describes / her.
. . ."[18] Although Creeley is vulnerable to romantic love, he
nourishes no illusions about the difficulties of maintaining it through
years of domesticity, and can be sardonic: "Let me say (in anger) that
since the day we were married / we have never had a towel / where
anyone could find it, / the fact. / Notwithstanding that I am not /
simple to live with. . . ."[19]

Many of Creeley's poems recount dreams, surreal situations and
the unease of nightmare. In "The World," he wants to reassure his
sleeping wife, and wakefully draws aside their bedroom curtains:

> The light, love,
> the light we felt then,
> greyly, was it, that
> came in, on us, not
> merely my hands or yours,
> or a wetness so comfortable,
>
> but in the dark then
> as you slept, the grey
> figure came so close
>
> and leaned over,
> between us, as you
> slept, restless, and
>
> my own face had to
> see it, and be seen by it,
> the man it was, your

> grey lost tired bewildered
> brother, unused, untaken—
> hated by love, and dead,
>
> but not dead, for an
> instant, saw me, myself
> the intruder, as he was not.
>
> I tried to say, it is
> all right, she is
> happy, you are no longer
>
> needed. I said,
> he is dead, and he
> went as you shifted
>
> and woke, at first afraid,
> then knew by my own knowing
> what had happened—
>
> and the light then
> of the sun coming
> for another morning
> in the world. [20]

The gray light of the comforting dawn becomes the gray shade of his wife's dead brother, then the sunlight of the real world. This poem is calm, subtle as a mezzotint, yet we are convinced of its uncanny reality. There is also a fine counterpoint, frequent in Creeley, between the wide implications of the title and the highly individual situation.

Water is an apt metaphor for Creeley's emotions and ideas, as they flow through diverse structures searching for a concrete form. "Trying to think of / some way out, the / rocks of thought / which displace, / dropped in / the water, / much else. / So life is / water, love also. . . ." [21] Creeley is preoccupied with numbers, particularly in his later poems such as "Numbers for Robert Indiana." This seems to indicate a search for the definite in a poetry which has become increasingly abstract and devoid of detail.

Creeley's poems were refreshingly modest; but for a while after 1966 they became increasingly sparse and at worst skimpy and petty. How lean can a poem be before it reaches vanishing point? Creeley was heavily influenced by Williams and his credo "no ideas but in things" (which became an axiom of Projective Verse). In his early work Creeley seemed to "misread" this as "no ideas but in feelings." But if "FORM IS NEVER MORE THAN AN EXTENSION OF CONTENT" then after 1966 that form so collapsed that we must wonder what became of the content that had previously undergirded it. Creeley's language became cruder, flatter and quite dull. The rationale for minimal language in poetry is that its non-specific nature allows the reader to interpret a poem in a variety of ways in the light of his or her own experience. But most of Creeley's later poems became so banal that they evoked no response in the reader. There was a tone of contrived condescension and indifference to the reader, which was perhaps the battle-fatigue of years of teaching. Some people (notably those under thirty) blamed the decline in Creeley's poetry on his turning forty in 1966. But except for serious illness or senility (which strikes some poets regardless of age), real poets no more retire after a certain age than monarchs do. For every Rimbaud who abandons poetry before twenty-one there are dozens of poets whose best work is done in their mature years.

Fortunately, about 1977 there was a turning point in Creeley's work which produced the poems published in *Later* in 1980. Maturity has brought new subjects: growing old and dying. At fifty-five, Creeley has reached an age when people he knows begin to die, and there are several poems dedicated to dead friends and a particularly moving one about his late mother "Four Years Later." Although concerned with mortality, Creeley's latest poems are not morbid and conclude with a simple hope and acceptance of the everyday. He has made a welcome return to the flowing tension of his best work, which is small in scale but wide in implication.

Edward Dorn, a student of Charles Olson's for several years, inherited his mentor's search for an intensely local yet universal place to be celebrated in poetry. Olson easily chose his hometown of Gloucester for his epic, but Dorn had difficulty settling. Born in Villa Grove, Illinois, after studying at Black Mountain he has taught and held fellowships at various places, including Santa Fe, New Mexico; Pocatello, Idaho; Kent, Ohio; and Colchester, Essex. If Olson's preoccupation (on the evidence of *Maximus*) might be paraphrased "no ideas but in *place*," then Dorn's misreading might be "sure, no ideas but in place, but I haven't got a place."

> So there is a dream story
>   of a true enough man named Pedro
> "a man without a country"
> in the cowering simplicity of the newspaper phrase
> it is reported he was a stowaway
> on the English cargo ship Oakbank 2 years ago
> but he has no papers and every country
> rejects him. He says he is a Brazilian.
> He will ply the seas, a captive there
> until he dies. His references do not exist.
> No Deans will welcome him. No housewives
> have come forth with a cup of coffee
> no workers will welcome him upon the job
> no greeting of any kind seems forthcoming. . . .
> His first name
> is all he has, always the sign of
> an acutely luckless man, his first name
> can be used by anyone. . . .
> He is the man we all are and yet he doesn't exist.
> He is the man we would all save with our tongues
> because we are secretly him.
> . . . qualified and eager young man
> or woman, fluent french and english
> would travel . . .[22]

Dorn's wanderings are partly a product of the university writer-in-residence system and partly a reflection of his own restlessness. His travels are also especially (though not exclusively) typical of a generation of young people who became nomads and searched for their identities in lands more remote than ever before. Not only hippie kids but average Americans tended to uproot themselves and move thousands of miles from their home towns. The elderly even formed trailer caravans.

Although he lived in England for several years, Dorn is emphatically American. In "Sousa" he sees "Great brass bell of austerity / and the ghosts of old picnickers / ambling under the box elder, where the

sobriety / was the drunkenness."[23] While he was nostalgic for the
simplicities of his farm childhood, Dorn, like other poets, was caught
in a dilemma in the mid-sixties: how could he celebrate America (after
the examples of Williams and Olson) while the Vietnam war was in
full spate and many intelligent young people were urging a complete
change in American society? Dorn's Americanism differs from
Pound's: Dorn doesn't look back on a Jeffersonian golden age (except
briefly in *North Atlantic Turbine*), nor does he analyze America's
problems with cranky economic theories. Dorn's political poems are
committed but refreshingly free of cant.

> This afternoon someone, an american
> from new york, spoke
> to me knitting his brows, of
> "the american situation" like
> wasn't it deplorable, a malignancy
> of the vital organs say News
> from nowhere. A mahogany sideboard of tastes.
> I knitted my brows too
> an old response
>   and tried to look serious
> Look like I was thinking of quote back home.
>
> Look like I *have* a home, pretend
> like anyone in the world
> I know where that is. And could
> if I chose, go there.
>
> I thought sure as hell
> he is going down
> the whole menu
>   Civil rights cocktail
>   Vietnam the inflexible entree
> oh gawd what will there be for pudding
> (not another bombe [24]

His laconic wit and puns rescue him from the smug self-righteousness
that pervades so much political verse of the sixties. The exact pitch of
ordinary American speech is well captured by Dorn. Although in
recordings he dutifully inhales and breaks breath as Olson dictated, on
the page Dorn's lines quietly assume their natural shape.

Dorn's feeling for America, unlike Olson's, is not centered on one small locality. But if there is any one area which compels his affection, it is the West, the mountainous West of Idaho and that archetypal American, the cowboy. "The cautious Gunslinger / of impeccable personal smoothness / and slender leather encased hands / folded casually / to make his knock, / will show you his map. / There is your domain."[25] Dorn has written a mock-epic, *Gunslinger*, with such wry satires of the Wild West as a talking, pot-smoking horse named Claude Lévi Strauss. The cowboy personifies Dorn's preoccupation with movement: not only is the cowboy constantly on the move himself, but also his job is to move along thousands of head of cattle. Dorn also uses technological subjects in his poems, such as astronauts and computers, which many of his contemporaries ignore.

Unfortunately, in Dorn's recent books—*Manchester Square* and *Hello, La Jolla*—the wandering bard has become a bored tourist, content with a few Polaroid snapshots. Dorn's method of evoking a place is based on an essentially American perspective (which he shares with Olson): the geology of a physical land which is relatively sparse in recorded human history. When he applies this method to an English place like Oxford it is inadequate to capture either the nuances of contemporary human behavior or the resonances of a rich historical past. Dorn seems to realize this failure and goes away sullenly. However, he has always been productive and has steadily advanced from the influences of Pound and Olson. Hopefully he will not only find his "spot," his particular locality, but also a "voice" that is entirely his own. "The cosmology of the floor of the Nation / The cosmology of finding your place. . . ."[26]

"Form is never more than the *revelation* of content."[27] So Denise Levertov revised one principle of Projective Verse, which Charles Olson had stated as "Form is never more than the extension of content." Levertov's conscious "misreading" of Projective Verse theory suited her view that the function of poetry is essentially sacerdotal, a device for revealing the worlds hidden beneath the everyday. "The lonely white / rabbit on the roof is a star / twitching its ears at the rain. . . . / Those who were sacred have remained so, / holiness does not dissolve, it is a presence / of bronze, only the sight that saw it / faltered and turned from it. / An old joy returned in holy presence."[28] It is

hardly surprising that this concept of poetry as revelation should un-
derlie Denise Levertov's work: her mother was descended from the
Welsh mystic Angel Jones of Mold; her father, although he had become an Anglican vicar, was descended from Schneour Zalman of
Ladie (d. 1813), the Rav of Northern White Russia, and he devoted
many years to a co-translation of *The Zohar*, the thirteenth-century
Jewish mystical "Book of Splendor." How many angels, multicolored
gems and cabbalistic beasts must have infused the front parlor of the
vicarage in Ilford, England, where Denise Levertov grew up. This
sense of splendor is apparent in her finely drawn nature poems, especially her early ones, such as "The Lagoon," in which the water
"draws the mind / down to its own depths / where the imagination
swims, / shining dark-scaled fish, / swims and waits, flashes, waits and
/ wavers, shining of its own light."[29] The dream-like, fragmentary
style of *The Zohar*, where disparate topics jostle each other until they
strike a spark of revelation, is echoed in the surreal images of Levertov's dream poems. "With eyes at the back of our heads / we see a
mountain / not obstructed with woods but laced / here and there with
feathery groves."[30]

Throughout Denise Levertov's poems there is a didactic tone (one
poem in *The Sorrow Dance* is even entitled "Didactic Poem"). And
sometimes her poems extend their implications as do parables or the
Hassidic stories she frequently cites in epigraphs. But her attempts to
give her poems a very broad meaning lead to problems in occasional
weaker ones: titles which are too abstract, disjointed from their poems;
limp verbs; and ineffectual endings.

Yet Levertov is far from other-worldly: the moral imperatives of
Hasidism find expression in left-wing political action. Her dead sister,
Olga, to whom she wrote several poems, was long active in socialist
causes; Denise Levertov's husband for many years was Mitchell Good-
man, a writer and radical activist. Politics dominate the books she
wrote after the mid-sixties such as *To Stay Alive*, which was written
while her husband was on trial with Dr. Benjamin Spock and other
war protesters, and which chronicles her participation in peace mar-
ches, with readings to raise money for revolutionary bookstores, and
describes atrocities in Vietnam. Much of this book, although indisputably sincere, is rhetoric and lacks the depth of perception that
enriches her earlier poems. In "Goodby to Tolerance" (1973) she

angrily rejects the liberal value of objective judgment. "We shan't meet again— / unless you leap it, leaving / behind you the cherished / worms of your dispassion, / your pallid ironies, / your jovial, murderous, / wry-humored balanced judgment. . . ."[31] Such a stance may have been necessary "to stay alive" in the turbulent sixties which so personally involved her. But the general effect on her poetry was to narrow consciousness and oversimplify images as she hurried on in slangy prose. Certainly a loosening of her early somewhat starchy tone had been needed, and she cites her move to America in 1948 and her association with the Black Mountain poets as vital in finding new rhythms of speech. Yet occasionally she stirs in trendy phrases such as "Amerikan," "tightassed" and "ripped off" which are now dated clichés. It may well have been a decade when, as she said, "There comes a time when only anger / is love."[32] Yet only anger is not poetry. The reader who comes to her Vietnam verses already repelled by the sheer horror of that war will not have his or her conviction changed or widened by them; the reader who may have felt the war was justified will turn the page when faced with the familiar propaganda, which is less vivid than the gory news films that flickered over millions of supper tables in those years. Denise Levertov is only one of many poets who were not completely successful on the topic of Vietnam; but they preferred to risk literary failure rather than moral dishonor. Feminist issues also entered Levertov's poetry in the late sixties, and gave it a new candor and strength.

Fortunately Denise Levertov is convinced that "We need a poetry not of *direct statement* but of *direct evocation:* a poetry of hieroglyphics, of embodiment, incarnation; in which the personages may be of myth or of Monday, no matter, if they are of the living imagination."[33] Her work may be seen as a struggle to harmonize opposites, just as on the cabbalistic Tree of Life the forceful lights of judgment and mercy oppose and balance each other. In her books before *The Sorrow Dance* (1968) the tension ran between the hidden and the revealed. She has also written about the struggle to contain diverse roles within one woman in poems such as "In Mind," which contrasts a kind and clean girl who has no imagination with a "moon-ridden girl / or old woman . . . / who knows strange songs— / but she is not kind."[34] The poet also contains within one person both Jacob and the angel he battles with.

When love, exaltation, the holy awe
of Poetry entering your doors and lifting you
on one finger as if you were a feather
fallen from its wings, grasp you, then your face
is luminous. I saw the angel
of Jacob once, alabaster, stone and not stone,
incandescent.
That look, the same,
illumines you, then.
                              But when
hatred and a desire of vengeance
make you sullen, your eyes grow smaller,
your mouth turns sour, a heaviness
pulls the flesh of your poet's face
down, makes it a mask
of denial.[35]

Denise Levertov's struggle to reconcile contraries in her poems charges
them with a tension that almost always fascinates the reader: her intelligence is kindled with passion, her mysticism balanced by political
engagement.

Robert Duncan's poetry is the most adventurous, splendid and un-
derestimated of the Black Mountain group. Indeed to place him
within any momentary "school" is inadequate, for he is allied with
much older traditions and disciplines. In many of his lyrics we can
hear echoes of the Greek Anthology, yet Duncan's idiom is unmistakably modern. Although many poets have influenced Duncan (he lists
Stein, Lawrence, Pound, H. D., Williams, Marianne Moore, Stevens
and Edith Sitwell), he has adapted their styles to his own purposes. He
is poised between passion and form, like a dancer:

                              This
would-have-been feverish cool excess of
                    movement makes
      each man   hit the pitch   co-
                    ordinate.

Lovely their feet pound the green solid meadow.
                    The dancers

> mimic flowers—root stem stamen and petal
>   our words are,
> our articulations,   our
>   measures.

> It is the joy that exceeds pleasure. . . .
>   I remember only the truth.
>   I swear by my yearning.

> *You have conquered the yearning*, she said
> *The numbers have enterd your feet.* . . .[36]

Duncan's balance between sensuality and measure is not confined to early lyrics, but has continued to enrich his mature work.

The act of writing itself is a subject which has often engaged Duncan, both in individual poems and in long sequences such as *The Structure of Rime*. His awareness and insight displayed in his critical writings have few if any equals among "experimental" poets writing today. Duncan's intelligence also leads to poems that have profound depths and arcane obscurities. At times these hermetic references can be an almost insurmountable barrier to the reader, particularly as there is as yet no extensive critical exposition of Duncan's symbolic system. Occult references are no hindrance, however, if the poem itself is fascinating enough to entice the reader to discover their sources. Like Yeats's mystical systems, Duncan's arcane images are an amalgamation of Rosicrucianism, theosophy, Lurianic Cabbalism and assorted alchemical texts. Their accepted meanings can often be found in reference books if the reader is alert. For example, many of the perplexing images in *The Structure of Rime* are accepted symbols of alchemical transformation and initiation: the black demon king of VII represents *nigredo*, putrefaction and mock death; the moon in the next poem evokes the following stage of *albedo*, the white stone, self-examination and rebirth. These usages were foreshadowed in preceding poems. Yet merely finding the accepted meaning of an occult symbol will not completely distill the poem's gold. As Duncan himself says: "(I mean to force up emblems again into these passages of a poetry, passages made conglomerate, the pyramid that dense, a mountain, immovable; cut ways in it then and trick the walls with images establishing space and time for more than the maker knows he acknowledges, in it)."[37] These occult symbols are important indicators of

Duncan's belief in harmonious parallels between worlds: "Wherever we watch, concordances appear. / What I call magic proceeds from the heart: / the blood there in its courses / has pulse in this longing. O melody / immaculately carrying pulses on this longing![38] "What opulence of my temper does not advance its charges? / What intricate shifting of mood in the world's weather / does not show cosmic affinities?"[39] Writing for Duncan is a sacred act, the very letters of the alphabet capable of creating worlds as they were for the Cabbalists. No one is more aware than Duncan that an excess of hermetic lore can become "*too too* much of beauty in this beauty," and he pokes fun (with more than a hint of self-mockery) at Eric Satie's mystic master, Sar Péladan.[40]

Although some critics in the past have cited Duncan's candid descriptions of homosexuality as an impediment, I do not think the majority to today's sophisticated readers are disturbed by some of his explicitly physical poems. There has always been homosexual poetry, of course, but with the advent of Gay liberation movement in the late sixties, many Gay poets wrote more openly and strongly about their feelings without the need for the verbal evasions of the past. Duncan is capable of a counterpoint of the sublime and squalid, as in "Night Scenes". At his strongest, Duncan's love lyrics transcend the person he intended them for and strike a sympathetic response in readers of any sexual persuasion.

> Again you have shown me the door.
> I have been thrown out. "Go to hell,"
> and there the open door.
> Where I long to go into the open. . . .

> "I go where I love and where I am loved."
> When you say go,
> I go. I obey. I obey. . . .
> Am I on the brink of happiness?
> Am I on the brink of panic?

> Not even love or not-love
> seems significant
> when I consider
> the panic with which I walk
> towards the house of friends.[41]

Is Duncan's style a revived Romanticism or radically new? Although some of his attitudes are similar to those of the Romantic poets, his way of using words is emphatically modern. Olson's influence on Duncan's typography has waned, but the Black Mountain idea of the poem as a simultaneous "field" has remained important in Duncan's work. He consciously uses the methods of a collagist (his companion of many years, Jess Collins, is an artist who has done many collages), and in "A Poem Beginning with a Line by Pindar" Duncan says, "Pindar's art, the editors tell us, was not a statue but a mosaic, an accumulation of metaphor."[42] This also true of Duncan's own work. Although he agrees with the concept of the poem as a "field," Duncan's intelligence and sense of proportion are always active, and his poems are by no means "cut-ups" or neo-Dada word salads. Duncan's "misreading" of Projective Verse theory might be phrased as "Yes, the poem is a field, but it is a field I shall return to again and again and leave marked by my circular dance." Sometimes this mosaic or "field" approach can mar Duncan's poems when their endings do not seem inevitable and there are several premature denouements before a verbose poem closes. Occasionally Duncan feels compelled to interrupt willfully the flow of a poem, or as he says: "I attempt the discontinuities of poetry. To interrupt all sure course of my inspiration."[43] Naturally he has more room to maneuver in the poem as a field over the course of the long sequences which he frequently composes, and he is adroit at varying his styles to keep each section fresh. At their most successful these sequences revolve several images, like beach pebbles tumbling in a gem polisher, until they reveal unsuspected lusters.

A poem, for Duncan, is a natural thing, splendid or awkward as a spawning salmon or a moose:

> The poem
> feeds upon thought, feeling, impulse,
>   to breed itself,
> a spiritual urgency at the dark ladders leaping. . . .
>
> salmon not in the well where the
>   hazelnut falls
> but at the falls battling, inarticulate,
>   blindly making it.

This is one picture apt for the mind.

A second: a moose painted by Stubbs,
where last year's extravagant antlers
         lie on the ground.
The forlorn moosey-faced poem wears
         new antler-buds,
         the same,

   "a little heavy, a little contrived,"

    his only beauty to be
         all moose.[44]

Duncan's singularly luminous style discovers a radiance in personal events (without ignoring their reality and intimacy) and reflects in the reader "a joy that exceeds pleasure."

Charles Olson's personal influence and his Projective Verse theory are the common factors uniting the Black Mountain poets. This theory's "usableness in practice" varied among them, and each of them altered it to serve his or her needs. Olson may have sounded like a patent medicine man hawking his cure-all Projective Verse as if it were Indian snake oil (although it was the same old New England cod liver oil), but for some poets Projective Verse was an invigorating spring tonic. The new openness and energy generated by the Black Mountain poets have ensured that, in Olson's words, "what does not change / is the will to change."[45]

4

"Whitman's Wild Children": The Beats

The Beat poets erupted into the American literary scene like a cesspool exploding under a Sunday-school picnic. Never has a group of new poets caused more outrage, become so well known even among the non-literary public or attracted so many imitators as did the Beats in the late fifties. Before we tackle individual Beat poets, we should consider a basic question raised by the Beat movement's notoriety: "What sort of person is a poet and what is his place in American society?"

To a casual observer, the Beats appeared to be hairy, horny outcasts who rebelled against "square" society and rejected its values. Certain Beat poets wallowed with glee in such outrageous subjects as heroin, boy whores, and every imaginable body opening and excretion: ". . . who copulated ecstatic and insatiate with a bottle of beer a sweetheart a package of cigarettes a candle and fell off the bed, and continued along the floor and down the hall and ended fainting on the wall with a vision of ultimate c . . . and come eluding the last gyzym of consciousness. . . ."[1] The bohemian rebel poet has become a familiar figure who reacts against a restrictive, unimaginative society, as America certainly was in the fifties. Long ago, Tiresias had warned King Pentheus not to chain Dionysus: "You rely on force; but it is not force that governs human affairs. . . . Self-control in all things depends on our own natures."[2] The English Romantic poets rejected the literary and political establishment of the early nineteenth century. Walt Whitman (who was venerated by the Beats) had shocked the Boston literary Brahmins with his sexual candor and long unrhymed lines. The French Symbolists—Baudelaire, Rimbaud and Verlaine—denounced bourgeois society and helped create "la vie bohème," the way of life in the Paris artists' quarter which became popularly known through Puccini's opera. The Paris of the twenties, host to expatriate writers such as Hemingway, Fitzgerald and Stein, also became fixed in the American fancy as a place where artists led wild lives far from rural America. Greenwich Village in New York City had had a similar reputation for some years. So the emergence of San Francisco as a center of Beat "bohemia" in the fifties (and of "flower power" in 1967) was part of a familiar pattern: to the average American, poets were segregated in a distant urban ghetto where they were thought to drink, screw around and douse themselves with drugs. But the price of the writers' freedom and originality was believed to be poverty, squalor and early death—the slum conditions which suburbia was created to prevent. This bohemian image of the poet, which had begun with the Romantics, was firmly cemented in popular thinking by 1956. That was the year Elvis Presley first vibrated over nationwide television, sending millions of teenagers into shrieks and spasms of delight and getting their horrified parents all shook up. Adolescent rebellion was no longer merely "going through a phase"; rebellion itself had become a life-style. In that same year Allen Ginsberg's *Howl* was published, provoking a lawsuit for obscenity and selling out as fast as it could be printed. The Beat movement, unlike other "bohemias" in the past, had extensive coverage on TV and radio in magazines and paperbacks.

Not only did the Beats reject the values of fifties American society, but they frequently rejected Western civilization and derided formal education; what mattered was experience of the world, which could typically be gained by wanderings "on the road." This theme of travel occurs again and again in Beat verse, (rather like the *Drang nach Süden*, the "urge to travel South" which the German Romantics had felt). Although the Beats claimed experience was better than erudition, they justified this reliance on immediate reality by readings in Sartre, Camus and existentialism, then at the height of its popularity. Literary apprenticeship, whether to living or dead writers, was also repudiated by the Beats, who felt that "if my heart-mind is shapely . . . the song will also be shapely."[3] The inspiration of the moment, not intricate revision, was the ideal for writing: breathless, brief periods of composition, often of a day only, were proudly noted at the end of many Beat verses. Their language was colloquial, often coarse and sometimes adamantly obscene by the standards of the day.

In some ways the Beats were introspective: a poet's surreal fantasies might dictate images in a kind of "automatic writing"; drugs were used to liberate parts of the mind repressed by puritanical social conventions; and Eastern mystical religions which stressed expansion of the individual consciousness were extremely popular. Although there are parallels here with nineteenth-century Romanticism, particularly Blake's, the Beats' romanticism was *urban* rather than rural, and celebrated aspects of American cities which the English poets would have found repulsive. Yet the Beats' apparent introspection was deceptive: personal emotions and events were not only to be made public, but were idealized as a style for others to imitate. At the Berkeley Poetry Conference in 1965 Allen Ginsberg declared: "Private is Public and Public is how we behave." Life-styles were highly important to the Beats who made them the basis for deciding who was "cool" enough to be included in their literary subculture. Like jazz, Beat poetry favored improvisation, discordant juxtaposition of subjects, public performance and the strident, egocentric voice of the individual. Beat slang was not original, but borrowed from blacks, particularly jazz musicians. However, the Beats used this language without the rich cultural context which had kept the words alive and renewed them for black musicians. The Beat vocabulary was extremely limited and all too easily parodied not only by foes but by camp followers. Blacks were idealized by the Beats as cool, amoral, living for kicks and able to have musical orgasms as easily as breathing (i.e. happy darkies with "natcheral rhythm"). This image of blacks was a fantasy of the white Beats who tried to do all the things they imagined blacks were doing— just as other whites relished the media picture of "dirty, depraved Beatniks" who slurped all the fruit that was forbidden to suburbanites.

Despite the Beats' pose as outsiders in language, morals and appearance, they were still very involved with square society and adroit at hustling publicity. Not only did they persistently attempt to outrage society (which is impossible to do without communicating in some form with people who can be shocked), but in many of their rhetorical poems (written in simple forms which even squares could understand) the Beats assumed a prophetic role, and earnestly told society how it should improve itself. Many Beat poets had long had left-wing sympathies, and they became more outspoken as nuclear testing and other issues grew more urgent in the late fifties and early sixties. It was not only a political revolution that Beat poets such as Allen Ginsberg and Gary Snyder advocated, but a complete shake-up of society's consciousness. The Beats, despite their boasts of wickedness, were intense moralists: only those with a fierce conscience would find it stimulating to catalogue "sins" of drugs and sex.

The Beats may have been right to condemn fifties America, and they were certainly brave to defy the literary establishment. Yet as we read the Beats' jeremiads against America we must keep in mind that the bardic/prophetic role they wanted was as firmly in the mainstream of American society as any American preacher's.

No Beat poet embodies the predicament of the poet in American society more vividly than Allen Ginsberg. In "America" he exhorts his country with exasperation and defiance:

> America I've given you all and now I'm nothing.
> America two dollars and twentyseven cents January 17, 1956.
> I can't stand on my own mind.
> America when will we end the human war?
> Go fuck yourself with your atom bomb.
> I don't feel good don't bother me.
> I won't write my poem till I'm in my right mind.
> America when will you be angelic?
> When will you take off your clothes? . . .
> America when I was seven momma took me to Communist
>   Cell meetings they sold us garbanzos a handful per ticket
>   a ticket costs a nickel and the speeches were free every-
>   body was angelic and sentimental about the workers it
>   was all so sincere you have no idea what a good thing
>   the party was in 1935 Scott Nearing was a grand old
>   man a real mensch Mother Bloor made me cry I once
>   saw Israel Ampter plain. Everybody must have been a
>   spy.[4]

Ginsberg is flashing a red flag at the bull of McCarthyism and the timid cows of conformity that trod down innovation in fifties America.

Despite his denunciation of America, Ginsberg never considers permanent exile. In "A Supermarket in California" he thinks of Walt Whitman: "I saw you, Walt Whitman, childless, lonely old grubber, / poking among the meats in the refrigerator and eyeing the grocery boys. . . . / Will we stroll dreaming of lost America of love past / blue automobiles in driveways, home to our silent cottage? / Ah, dear father, graybeard, lonely old courage-teacher, / what America did you have . . .?"[5] Locked into America like a wrestler who cannot let go of his antagonist, Ginsberg shuttles across the land addressing poems to such unreceptive places as Wichita.

Poetry for Ginsberg is a means toward the goals of radical politics and a complete change in culture. He demands that society invest him with a bard/prophet's mantle: "I continued in a violent / and messianic voice, inspired at / last, dominating the whole room."[6] "I suddenly turned aside in San Francisco, unemployment compensation leisure, to follow my romantic inspiration—Hebraic-Melvillian bardic breath."[7] Yet the America Ginsberg exhorts is a black shadowgraph of himself. His awareness of this trick played by his mind is one of the advantages he gains from his method of omnivorous inclusion. "It occurs to me that I am America. / I am talking to myself again."[8]

Ginsberg wants to be an American prophet, but unlike Whitman and Williams, whom he admires, Ginsberg is a self-mutilating prophet, similar to those priests in the ancient Middle East who gashed themselves in an effort to compel the gods to send rain for the crops. Ginsberg's self-loathing is expressed not only in his revulsion toward the America that represents himself, but also in his exposure of many embarassing aspects of himself and his family, particularly his mother: "One night, sudden attack—her noise in the bathroom—/ like croaking up her soul—convulsions and red vomit coming / out of her mouth—diarrhea water exploding from her behind /—on all fours in front of the toilet—urine running between / her legs—left retching on the tile floor smeared with her black feces—unfainted—."[9] The reader is repelled by these skeletons rummaged out of family closets, and even the most morbid curiosity finally tires of the repetitive prurience. Yet many readers dutifully plod on, because Ginsberg is adept at sticking in the barbed hooks of Jewish guilt. After all he's done for us, by demolishing the New Critics and bringing a new freedom to poetry, how can we be so ungrateful as to put his books down? To ignore him is to deny his suffering, to become identified with those anticom-

munist witch-hunters his mother dreaded and to side with Moloch, J.
Edgar Hoover and other assorted boogeymen. The reader also persists
out of hope for better things, encouraged by Ginsberg's passages of
compelling power, such as parts of "Kaddish."

Ginsberg states boldly the intention of his poetry: "the message is:
widen the area of consciousness." [10] His assumption of a bardic and
prophetic role is partly based on his own mystical experiences: ". . . I
went on to what my imagination believed true to Eternity (for I'd had
a beatific illumination years before during which I'd heard Blake's ancient voice & saw the universe unfold in my brain) . . . ." [11] Ginsberg has also attempted to widen his consciousness with a cornucopia
of licit and illicit drugs. (William Burroughs, long a friend of Ginsberg's, introduced him to both the drug and homosexual scenes.) Like
many other poets in the late fifties and early sixties, Ginsberg looked
East for inspiration and has traveled in India and Japan. References to
Hinduism and Buddhism proliferate in his poetry of the sixties: poems
are titled "sutras," assorted gods and goddesses are invoked and fragments of chants inserted.

The long poem "Kaddish" marks the high tide of Ginsberg's
achievement. "Kaddish" is a lament for and celebration of his mother,
who died after years of physical and mental suffering. The terrible
whirlwind of Naomi Ginsberg's paranoia, degeneration and death is so
devastating that her son must grip onto his poem lest his own sanity be
swept away as his mother simulataneously engulfs and deserts him. He
has no hand free for coy hipster waves to his friends or to thumb his
nose at the establishment. Ginsberg has said his intention was to write
"a death-prayer imitating the rhythms of the Hebrew Kaddish." [12]
(The litugical Jewish Kaddish, incidentally, was not written in Hebrew
but in Aramaic, the vernacular, so that it might be understood by
all.) [13] Although Ginsberg approximately transcribes the liturgy in the
first two lines of the "Hymmnn" section of "Kaddish," he soon departs
from it, when it says "though he is above all the praises, hymns and
adorations which men can utter." Ginsberg's subsequent naturalistic
images and staccato rhythms owe more to Ray Charles and black re-
vivalists than to rabbis. The prayer ends: "May the Most High, source
of perfect peace, grant peace to us . . ."; near the close of his poem,
Ginsberg repeats a benediction from his mother's last letter: "The key
is in the sunlight at the window in the bars the key is in the sunlight." [14] By his own standard, widening the area of consciousness

(which is the same one I proposed), "Kaddish" is a very good poem indeed. It relentlessly transforms a squalid family embarrassment into an epic which embraces every beloved parent who has disintegrated into a death without dignity and which leaves a key for the living in the bars which have become bars of sunlight.

Since "Kaddish" Ginsberg's verse has declined miserably. Typical of his recent output is *Iron Horse*, a long poem describing Ginsberg masturbating in a train traveling across America carrying soldiers who have fought in Cambodia. Among the poem's baggage are news clippings, a transliteration of an ethnic chant (possibly Mojave?), shards of pop culture and pronouncements such as: "The delicate chemical brain changes / Aethereal sensations / Muladhara sphincter up through mind aura / Sahasrarapadma promise / another univers—." [15] This is a lugubrious parody of Ginsberg's earlier work and not even City Lights' imaginative design can redeem the book from ghastliness. This long poem is a metaphor for Ginsberg's poetic activity in recent years: rushing across America jerking off, grabbing bits of gossip and news like plastic-wrapped sandwiches.

But Ginsberg is too important a poet to abandon prematurely. The Beat ideals which led him into his predicament have also affected other poets, so it is worthwhile to explore some reasons for his recent failures. Along with his faith in his prophetic role goes a belief in the sacredness of his inspiration. Although he sometimes revises, many of Ginsberg's poems are rough drafts written at speed, often while he was stoned. For example, Ginsberg says of "The Sunflower Sutra": "composition time 20 minutes, me at desk scribbling, Kerouac at cottage door waiting for me to go off somewhere party . . . ." [16] There isn't anything wrong with poems written in a flash, as long as that flash is truly inspired. Great poems, such as Coleridge's "Kubla Kahn," have been known to arrive full blown (albeit incomplete). But "Sunflower Sutra" is far from a great poem: it is verbose, maudlin, repetitious and cranks out its simple-minded moral as clumsily as a fundamentalist sandwich board. Another hazard of the prophetic role is that it stakes the validity of poetry on the amount of social change it is able to cause. Although America has changed considerably since *Howl* was published in 1956, it certainly hasn't "taken off its clothes," as Ginsberg urged in "America," while some states still outlaw homosexuality and a national television network censors "the naughty bits" from *Monty Python's Flying Circus*. Ginsberg, the grit in the American oyster, has been co-opted, opaquely coated with a bohemian role until he is no longer abrasive but merely doing what we have come to expect. There have been some signs lately that even Ginsberg is finding the prophetic mantle a drag: "I'll get drunk & give no shit, & not be a Messiah."[17]

The validity of poetry itself is called into question by Ginsberg's version of Indian philosophy: "Not to believe in Poetry— . . . not to hang on to anything at all."[18] His anarchist attitude toward political forms is echoed in his anarchist attitude toward poetic forms, even his own: no sooner does he establish a pattern than he either abandons it or repeats it into boredom long after it is appropriate to what he is saying. "Conventional form is too symmetrical, geometrical, numbered and fixed—unlike to my own mind which has no beginning and no end, nor fixed measures of thought other than its own cornerless mystery."[19] Alongside his exuberant celebrations of basic life forces, Ginsberg is capable of a nihilistic, depressive, destructive impulse. The phrase "Blessed be Death!" and a cold-eyed vision of crows cawing over a bleak and empty graveyard end "Kaddish."

Some of Ginsberg's current difficulties may also stem from his lack of a critical perspective from which to assess his own work. Although he studied with Lionel Trilling at Columbia and was William Carlos Williams's protégé, for years Ginsberg has avoided and abominated most critics (with the occasional exception of Eric Mottram, who has long been an ardent advocate of Beat poets). Ginsberg's bitterness may be understandable, considering the deodorant the New Critics sprayed at him and his Beat friends, but Ginsberg's dislike of formal criticism also arises from the fact that his critical standards are based partly on life-stlyes and politics rather than on artistic integrity. ". . . The very thing which doesn't interest me in their prose & poetry & makes it a long confused bore?—all arty & by inherited rule & no surprised new invention—corresponding inevitably to their own dreary characters—because most of them have no character and are big draggy minds that don't *know* and just argue from abstract shallow moral principles in the void?"[20] How easy and pleasant the literary critic's lot would be if groovy people always wrote good poetry! But alas, ogres can sometimes sing like angels and the nicest people can churn out abysmal drivel.

The failures of Ginsberg's recent verse were latent in the techniques of his earlier work. The shock of profanity and obscene images

has worn off, both because our society is less prudish and because the
dirty words become less startling and obscene every time they are
repeated. Ginsberg never was as adept at reproducing ordinary speech
as Ed Dorn, for instance, or Gregory Corso; in Ginsberg's later poems
phrases intended to convey the Common Man are merely banal. The
lack of artifice which was effective in "Kaddish" robs a poem like "In
the Baggage Room at Greyhound" of subtlety and surprise despite its
acute observation. Unlike his vital, breathing, appendix-scars-and-all
portrait of his mother in "Kaddish," the characters in Ginsberg's later
poems are thin and impersonal.

Ginsberg tackles large-scale subjects: death and immortality; mili-
tary industrial complexes and paranoias just as grandiose; deviance;
madness; and mysticism. It is not alone the scope of these subjects
which defeats him (for in "Kaddish" he manages an extraordinarily
difficult topic), but also his impatience with form, analysis and re-
working, none of which fit in with his much-publicized life-style.
Some hint of a change to come, however, might be seen in *Sad Dust
Glories* (1975). Written during a summer in the woods while Ginsberg
helped build a house, these poems are slight, but represent a fresh attempt to get to grips with the actual realities that surround him and are
a good omen for his future work. *Mind Breaths* (1977) also experiments with different forms and sometimes attempts to break out of his
stereotyped *persona*.

Publicity and the media are also to blame for Ginsberg's decline:
they have marketed him as the benign, bearded Colonel Sanders of
the counterculture, and he has obliged with a product that is predictable, tepid and widely available. Extensive public readings have also
shaped Ginsberg's work; we shall consider their influence on poetry in
general at the end of this chapter. Ginsberg has grumbled about the
onslaught of publicity in a witty poem, "I Am a Victim of Telephone," but his awareness of its dangers has not prevented it from
damaging his poetry. He has tried to use his prominence to help other
poets and has generously given his time to many causes. Some critics
have blamed Ginsberg's decline on the depletion of his resources of
feeling, since his successful early poems were highly autobiographical.
But Ginsberg has not grown insensitive with age, since even to his
thousands of casual acquaintances he can be warm and compassionate. At the Albert Hall poetry jamboree in London in 1965 Ginsberg read "Who to Be Kind To." His admirers have been too kind to

Ginsberg, who could be one of the major poets of our time but who has been squandering his time on feeble verses instead. It is inevitable that Ginsberg should be spoiled with kindness, since by clearing a channel for others he acted like an icebreaker ship—noisy, crude, but sturdy enough to survive the icebergs of American society.

The term "beat" was first used widely by Jack Kerouac, who said it was short for "beatific." "Beat" also meant broken down, weary, oppressed, and referred to the syncopated beat of jazz. Kerouac first met Allen Ginsberg and William Burroughs at Columbia University in 1944, and (with the later addition of Gregory Corso) this coterie became the core of the Beat movement. Kerouac's influence was largely through his friendships and popular novels, rather than his verse, which is thin and repetitive.

Gregory Corso's background fitted the Beat role of outsider: he was born in Greenwich Village; when his young Italian parents' marriage broke up they left him in an orphanage. Reform schools and juvenile delinquency followed. But in 1950 he met Ginsberg, who introduced him to other Beat writers. Some of them took Corso to Harvard and Radcliffe, where he made friends with the students and was first published by the *Harvard Advocate*. Like many of the Beats, Corso was fascinated by the forbidden and criminal, and his troubled background is reflected as a streak of violence in some of his early poems, such as "Greenwich Village Suicide," "At the Morgue" and "Last Night I Drove a Car":

> . . . not knowing how to drive
>   not owning a car
> I drove and knocked down
>   people I loved
>   . . . went 120 through one town.
>
> I stopped at Hedgeville
>   and slept in the back seat
>   . . . excited about my new life.[21]

Although Corso could write tough city poems, one of his favorite poets was Shelley, whose influence may be seen in the plush prosody of

"Amnesia in Memphis" and in the romantic "The Last Warmth of Arnold." Corso handles surreal images more skillfully than some other Beat poets and often uses them very wittily, as in "Marriage":

God what a husband I'd make! Yes, I should get married!
So much to do! like sneaking into Mr Jones' house late at night
and cover his golf clubs with 1920 Norwegian books
Like hanging a picture of Rimbaud on the lawnmower
Like pasting Tannu Tuva postage stamps
all over the picket fence
Like when Mrs Kindhead comes to collect for the Community Chest
grab her and tell her There are unfavourable omens in the sky!
And when the mayor comes to get my vote tell him
When are you going to stop people killing whales!
And when the milkman comes leave him a note in the bottle
Penguin dust, bring me penguin dust, I want penguin dust— . . .[22]

Here the poet is indeed part of American society, but he lives in suburbia only as a comic saboteur of its complacency. At his best, Corso has a knack of giving his poems, which have a casual surface, unexpected depths of perception, as in "Man Entering the Sea, Tangier." The man retraces the amphibians' evolutionary path:

That curious warm all too familiar
as when frogs from fish kicked
and fins winged flew
and whatever it was decided lungs
and a chance above the sea

He would it nothing more
than a holiday's dip
yet there he is
millions of years that are legs,
back into that biggest & strangest of wombs. . . .[23]

San Francisco was in many ways the focus to the Beat Movement. World War II camps for conscientious objectors had brought many dissidents and left-wing activists into the state. Writers such as Henry Miller and Kenneth Rexroth had long made their homes in Big Sur, and California had had a strong regional literature for some years. At the Six Gallery in 1956 Kenneth Rexroth organized a series of readings by Robert Duncan, Brother Antoninus, Philip Lamantia, Lawrence Ferlinghetti, Gary Snyder and several new arrivals to San Francisco—Allen Ginsberg, Philip Whalen and Gregory Corso. It was at one of these readings that Ginsberg first recited "Howl," which attracted publicity for the Beat movement, or as some preferred to call it, the "San Francisco Renaissance." Another energy center was Lawrence Ferlinghetti's City Lights bookstore. It stocked an extensive range of avant-garde paperbacks and the books of its own press, which started in 1955 to publish many of the Beat poets, often for the first time. Ferlinghetti wrote of San Francisco:

>   I see the sea come in
>   over South San Francisco
>   and the island of the city
>   truly floated free at last
>   never really a part of America
>   East East and West West
>   and the twain met long ago
>   in "the wish to pursue what lies beyond
>   the mind"
>   and with no place to go but In. . . .[24]

Ferlinghetti's own work covers a wide range of topics and techniques. A painter as well as a poet, he first became well known for A Coney Island of the Mind and an antinuclear broadside, "Tentative Description of a Dinner to Promote the Impeachment of President Eisenhower." He is skilled at delivering his messages with incisive wit, as a recent invective addressed to his poet friends shows:

>   . . . We have seen the best minds of our generation
>   destroyed by boredom at poetry readings.
>   Poetry isn't a secret society,
>   It isn't a temple either.
>   Secret words & chants won't do any longer. . . .
>   All you poetry workshop poets
>   in the boondock heart of America,
>   All you house-broken Ezra Pounds,

All you far-out freaked-out cut-up poets, . . .
All you pay-toilet poets groaning with graffitti,
All you A-train swingers who never swung on birches, . . .
All you bedroom visionaries
and closet agitpropagators, . . .
All you den mothers of poetry,
All you zen brothers of poetry, . . .
All you suicide lovers of poetry, . . .
Where are Whitman's wild children
where are the great voices speaking out. . . .[25]

Although Ferlinghetti has never written formal criticism, in his role as editor of City Lights he has been influential in forming the tastes of a generation of poetry readers. His wit is at the service of a surrealist's topsy-turvy vision, an apparently crazy response to a society that was often threatening and irrational. He had studied at the Sorbonne for several years and wrote his doctoral dissertation on "The City in Modern Literature."

Ferlinghetti's sense of humor (sometimes similar to Kenneth Patchen's whimsy) and his balance usually keep even his most surreal poems from disintegrating into gibberish. Also, Ferlinghetti's poems are quite structured, both as wholes and line by line, with devices such as internal rhyme. He takes chances with repeated phrases and puns and the result is occasionally maudlin. Ferlinghetti comprehends nature in terms of the city, and it is in these poems of urban romanticism that he is at his best.

> Sound of trains in the surf
>   in the subways of the sea
> And an even greater undersound
>   of a vast confusion in the universe
> a rumbling and a roaring
>   as of some enormous creature turning
>   under sea & earth. . . .[26]

LeRoi Jones, the black poet and playwright, was often associated with the Beat poets in the late fifties, but his work took a divergent path which underlines an essential difference between black poetry (which the Beats admired and sometimes tried to imitate) and Beat poetry. There is a long history of black poetry in America, beginning at least as early as 1746 with Lucy Terry's verses about an Indian raid; in 1760 Jupiter Hammon's poems were published and became widely known. Black poets continued to publish throughout the nineteenth century, particularly in New Orleans; the "renaissance" of the 1920s saw the emergence of a significant number of black poets such as Langston Hughes. Inexpensive recordings of the blues became widely available; the wit, compression and complex reversals of feelings in their lyrics influenced black (and white) poets. Black poetry began to reach a wider audience with Gwendolyn Brooks's first book in 1945 and Langston Hughes's anthology *The Poetry of the Negro* in 1949. From the early fifties onward, new black writers found outlets in a number of magazines such as *Umbra*, *CLA Journal* and *Free Lance*. Dudley Randall's Broadside Press also became a focus for black writers.

LeRoi Jones founded *Yugen* magazine in 1958, and its early issues featured such Beat poets as Ginsberg, Kerouac and Corso. As the black consciousness movement grew, it altered Jones's own work dramatically. The poems of his first period have the relaxed, hip cadences of a jazz player stoned on pot; there's an occasional discord or snarl, but it all seems part of the act. In the early seventies Jones divorced his Jewish wife, changed his name to Imamu Amiri Baraka and tried to banish all "white" elements (which he now detested) from his poetry. His more recent poems are abrasive, specifically political and written in unmistakable dialect.

At this time, black poets were under pressure to satisfy two obligations, social and artistic, which sometimes conflicted for priority. There was also the temptation of relatively easy publication, as radical chic replaced literary judgment on the part of some white publishers. A number of vibrant black poets used these pressures to produce strong poems without going to the same extremes as Jones/Baraka. Ishmael Reed, for instance, specializes in a crazy, surreal satire, which no one—white, black, red or yellow—can hide from. Some black poets wanted to be read as *poets* first and foremost, and resented the label "black" as another kind of segregation and stereotyping. Almost all black poets, however, have found that the experience of being black is an imperative subject for poetry. Like the Beats, black poets felt a need to discover the place of the poet in society, but for them there was the added anger and hurt at the injustices suffered by merely being born black (let alone a poet) in America.

Reading Gary Snyder after reading some other Beat poets is like breathing pine-tinged mountain air after city fumes. Yet his connections with the other Beats are more than accidents of geography and acquaintance: they share an interest in Buddhism, a preference for experience rather than Western education and an earthy frankness. Gary Snyder was born in San Francisco in 1930, grew up on a farm in Oregon and has worked at various times as a seaman and a logger. While laying a cobblestone trail for packhorses through the Sierras, he asked old Roy Marchbanks what he was doing. "Riprapping," was the reply.

> Lay down these words
> Before your mind like rocks. . . .
> Solidity of bark, leaf, or wall
>   riprap of things:
> Cobble of milky way,
>   straying planets,
> These poems, people,
>   lost ponies with
> Dragging saddles—
>   and rocky sure-foot trails. . . .[27]

"[Old Roy Marchbanks'] selection of natural rocks was perfect—the result looked like dressed stone fitting to hair-edge cracks. Walking, climbing, placing with the hands. I tried writing poems of tough, simple, short words, with the complexity far beneath the surface texture. In part the line was influenced by the five- and seven-character line Chinese poems I'd been reading, which work like sharp blows on the mind."[28] This "riprap" is indeed Snyder's technique. Like a brushstroke of Japanese calligraphy or a relaxed judo posture, the surface of his poems has a deceptive casualness yet they exert the power that is produced by practiced skill. His craft is without fussiness, his intensity without excess, like the clouds he describes: "WE/ pile up, pile up, our deep-mounting/pleasure in our richness/is not chaos."[29]

Snyder's finesse yields a lyric clarity, in which *things* themselves speak to us, each in its highly unique voice (like Rilke's *das Ding an sich,* "the thing itself," or Hopkins's "inscape").

> blueblack berry on a bush turned leaf-purple
>
> deep sour, dark tart, sharp
>   in the back of the mouth.
>
> in the hair and from head to foot
> stuck with seeds—burrs—
>   next summer's mountain weeds—
>
> a strolling through vines and grasses:
>
> into the wild sour.[30]

This authentic voice of living things and people sounds in the foreground of Gary Snyder's poems and distinguishes them from the urban romanticism of other Beat poets. Not only are Snyder's subjects rural rather than urban, but his primary concern is with these subjects themselves rather than his fantasies about them. He searches for the exact word with scholarly precision and, in fact, has studied linguistics.

Gary Snyder has achieved a more integrated understanding of Buddhism in his poetry than any other Beat poet. He spent a number of years in Japan and is an ordained Zen monk. By and large, the Buddhist terms he does employ can be partially understood from the context of his poems, although some terms can seem needlessly esoteric and abstract. Also occasionally irritating are his utopian pronouncements, a long series of which can be as boring as six days on nothing but brown rice. But, having enjoyed the freshness of Snyder's poetry, we can forgive him an occasional sermon.

Snyder has not gone out of his way to scream at straight American society, yet he is quite certain where he stands:

> Off the coast of Oregon
> The radio is full of hate and anger.
> "Teenagers! getting busted for shoplifting is no joke!"
>   phoney friendly cop voice,
> "The Ford Foundation is financing revolution—"

"Teach black people to have more self-respect
and they'll blame the white people more—"

> General Alarm
> When Bell Rings
> Go to Your
> Station

After midnight, the "clean time of night"
Rise to see the Morning Star.
Planting the peach tree, mopping the floor.
"we all
    worked hard to get ahead"
peach orchard turned roots-up and brush-piled
(the unspeakable U S government
cut down the Navajo peach trees
at Canyon de Chelly—). . . .[31]

Gary Snyder is a poet who has gone from strength to strength, and
we can continue to expect from him work as solid and rugged-textured
as a granite-cobbled mountain road.

At the beginning of this chapter I suggested that the most important
question the Beat movement prompts us to ask is: "What sort of person
is a poet and what is his place in American society?" Saul Bellow was
caustic:

> For after all Humbolt did what poets in crass America are
> supposed to do. He chased ruin and death harder than he had
> chased women. He blew his talent and his health and
> reached home, the grave, in a dusty slide. He plowed himself
> under. Okay. So did Edgar Allan Poe, picked out of the Bal-
> timore gutter. And Hart Crane over the side of a ship. . . .
> And poor John Berryman jumping from a bridge. For some
> reason this awfulness is particularly appreciated by business
> and technological America. The country is proud of its dead
> poets. It takes terrific satisfaction in the poets' testimony that
> the USA is too tough, too big, too much, too rugged, that

American reality is overpowering. And to be a poet is a
school thing, a skirt thing, a church thing. The weakness of
the spiritual powers is proved in the childishness, madness,
drunkeness, and despair of these martyrs. Orpheus moved
stones and trees. But a poet can't perform a hysterectomy or
send a vehicle out of the solar system. Miracle and power no
longer belong to him. So poets are loved, but loved because
they just can't make it here.[32]

One young poet who tried to follow the Beat life-style was d. a.
levy. Like some other Beat poets he had little formal education, used
frank language and was deeply involved in Eastern religions. But unlike other Beat poets, he didn't wander physically from his birthplace
of Cleveland, Ohio. After high school he joined the Navy briefly, and
by the time he was twenty-one he had started Renegade Press, which
published himself and other poets, including Paul Blackburn and
Charles Bukowski. Also on his publishing list was his magazine, *The
Marrahwanna Quarterly*. It was this and levy's public readings of his
poems which led the Cuyahoga County Grand Jury to indict him
secretly for "publishing and distributing obscene literature." On 5
January 1967 (the year of "flower-power") a warrant for levy's arrest
was issued, and he was jailed until his lawyer posted a $2,500 bond.
Judge Celebrezze (who was prominent in Cleveland politics) commented sarcastically: "Bail of $2,500 is not excessive for a great poet.
Maybe you should charge more than 89 cents [for your poetry]."[33]
That March levy was again arrested and charged on five counts of
"contributing to the delinquency of two minors" by reading poetry to
them in a coffee house in the basement of the Episcopal Cathedral, an
odd site for a den of iniquity. Although the *Cleveland Plain Dealer*
defended levy, his case festered on until February of the following year
when he pleaded no contest, was found guilty of "conduct tending to
cause the delinquency of minors" and was sentenced to six months in
the Warrensville Workhouse. After the Supreme Court obscenity rul-
ing in 1968, the charges against him were dropped. The Cleveland
authorities were expressing typically American terror, not only of poetry and imagination, but also of the impulses of the human unconscious. Cleveland's collective mind, flat as the prehistoric swamp upon
which the city sprawls, could not cope with levy, either as a poet or as

a deeply troubled young man. Cleveland was even more obtuse than the U.S. Navy, which had discharged levy after seven months for "manic depressive tendencies." On 24 November 1968, two friends discovered levy dead in his apartment, a .22 "deer rifle" by his side.

It is tempting to consider levy a heroic young martyr to provincial paranoia; some writers have fixed the sole blame on Cleveland (as representative of America) as simply as if they were reciting "Who Killed Cock Robin?"

Levy killed himself. Precisely why is impossible to determine, but he had been living on the edge of his nerves for some time. In his last long work, *Suburban Monastery Death Poem*, he wrote: "i cld tell you partly/why it happened/but you wouldnt believe me. . . ."[34] Friends described him as "especially lean, pale, and with an unusual capacity for stirring concerned feelings in others about issues. He also aroused anxious feelings in others about his own welfare, for he fluctuated somewhat violently between helplessness and independence.[35] Despite their ungrammatical tough-guy language, levy's poems reveal a confused vulnerability: "the total real meaning of this poem is, *i dont understand what its all about.* Everyone who knows about the light disappears when i ask them. . . ."[36]

> only ten blocks away
> from my total helplessness
> from my boredom enforced by the state
> they are looting stores
> trying to get televisions
> so they can watch the riots
> on the 11 pm news. . . .[37]

Levy's destructiveness extended not only to himself, but also to those who wanted to help him, and even to his poetry: he could write incisively for several lines but then dispelled the tension by rambling off on irrelevant topics or endlessly repeating the same grievances. Levy's decision to remain in Cleveland is startling and illogical: "At 17 I decided to stay in Cleveland. I made a commitment. Now I can't get out."[38] His reasons for not escaping were various (probably he wasn't aware of all of them himself), but it is possible that for him Cleveland was a panorama of the riots, pollution, conflicts and dead Indians inside his own head. Levy was like a man who, trapped in a waking nightmare of being eaten alive by a crocodile, searches for a real crocodile (which is less terrifying than his fantasy crocodile) and kicks it until it eats him alive.

Cleveland was all too willing to play crocodile and make levy's paranoid nightmares into reality. And not only Cleveland, but any number of places would have been antagonistic to levy. The struggle of the artist against his birthplace is an important theme of twentieth-century writers such as James Joyce, Sherwood Anderson and Edgar Lee Masters. Although poets are born in all sorts of places, they tend to escape from home as soon as possible. This exodus of creative writers becomes a vicious circle: practical, down-to-earth folks who have had no personal contact with writers accept media stereotypes of depraved bohemians, and try to stamp out any signs of artistic eccentricity in their youngsters. Talented kids realize they must get out, not only because of conformist pressures but because contacts with other writers and with publishers are elsewhere. The cultural ecology of a region thus becomes as unbalanced as that of a dead lake where pollution and algae have left no oxygen for fish.

Levy was determined to enlighten his hometown, even as the first vow of Buddhism is "Sentient beings are numberless, I vow to enlighten them all." Levy's efforts were in accord with Allen Ginsberg's attempt to levitate the Pentagon by chanting mantras. What the Beat poets were saying in effect was: "We are different, but we belong among you to show you a better way of being." Levy's decision to stay in the hostile environment of Cleveland and attempt to raise its consciousness may be seen as noble, quixotic, suicidal or silly, but it was typical of the mood of the sixties and the messianic aspects of the Beat movement.

Another factor in levy's suicide is the culture myth of the poet as a self-destructing bohemian.

> The mailman tells me he was a writer
> but he decided he liked to eat
> so much for how America keeps her
> writers in line
> if i have any courage
> next week i'll kill myself
> every week i tell myself that. . . .[39]

> . . . & everyone knows
> sleeping with the muse
> is only for young poets
> after you've been kept impotent
> by style & form & and words like "art"
> after being published by the RIGHT publishers
> and having all the right answers
> after youve earned the right to call yrself
> a poet   yr dead
> & lying on your back. . . .[40]

To succeed as a poet was to be dead. To live was cowardice and collusion with the system. This myth combined with the disturbed impulses in levy's mind and helped glamorize suicide. This poisonous image of the poet as brilliant but mad and destined for early death ought to be plunged in formaldehyde and locked away in some remote literary horror museum.

Levy was not a great poet; much of the time he was not even a good poet; yet he should have had more than twenty-six years to explore whatever gifts he had. Caught among the conflicting demands of his inner demons, Cleveland's paranoia and the Beat ideal (formed by those more talented and strong-willed than he was), levy could not survive.

Poetry readings have become so attractive to many contemporary poets, not only to the Beats, that it is worthwhile to pause a moment to consider their effects on poetry in general. Writing is a lonely business; writing poems is perhaps the loneliest task of all. No matter how private a poet may be, ultimately he writes poems in order to reach people, and young poets, especially, yearn to have readers respond to their efforts. Readings appear to offer poets the acknowledgment they so desire. In the fifties poetry readings were the only outlets for some newer poets; there were almost no presses or magazines which weren't dominated by the New Critics and there was no money available to start alternative presses. The present wave of American poetry readings began quietly in New York at the Young Men's Hebrew Association, grew after Dylan Thomas's tours and was widely publicized after Allen Ginsberg's obscenity trial in San Francisco in 1957. In the sixties poetry readings seemed to happen everywhere; although the atmosphere of the seventies was quieter, there are now well-established readings circuits and many venues open to beginners. For many poets readings provide a welcome source of income, may help to sell a few books and give poets a chance to meet people who are interested in their work. However, readings can also present some very serious problems, which some poets are unaware of. One poet described the visceral thrill she gets when giving readings with such heavy breathing and glazed eyes that I was tempted to suggest that what she needed was not an audience but an attentive lover. Unlike a book, a reading is undeniably a dramatic situation with the demands and rewards of that particular medium. Some poets satisfy the requirements of drama and their poems are enhanced by readings. But far too many poets are tempted by the need to entertain an audience; they write in language that instantly brings a laugh, a sigh, or a snort of righteous anger or use techniques like the mindless repetitions heard in television commercials. Readings often degenerate into cabaret, with the poet just another "personality" on parade. The audience at a reading is trapped (surprisingly few people ever get the courage to walk out, even on obviously awful verse). The book reader can control his pace; he can re-read a poem he likes or doesn't understand, or skip over one which may bore him. Readings also lack the visual dimension and interest of an illustrated book.

Are poetry readings a good thing? This question hinges on the answer to another question: which is more important, the poetry or the poet? No one would deny that poets need the financial support and encouragement that readings offer. And poets also need human contact with their audience—there have been far too many lonely, depressed American poets committing suicide in recent years. Yet the effects of readings on poetry itself have often been disastrous. There are a few poets who claim that readings have helped them to write better poems (Allen Ginsberg, for one, although the mediocrity of his later work would seem to contradict him), but for many poets the need to be entertaining at readings drives out all subtleties of language, texture, images or thought. This dominance of readings is one reason why many poems of the "second generation" New York poets collapse like soggy paper plates if you attempt to read them more than once. The poet matters, yes, but ultimately his poetry is what may outlast him; its development must be given priority. Fewer people go to readings now than in the sixties, which is a shame; because if both pc and audiences are candid with themselves about their motives an limitations, readings can be memorable and exciting.

What is the poet's place in American society? Up in front leading the singing, asserted the Beats. Since *Howl* was published in 1956, America has not become "angelic," yet there has been a widespread shift in what is permitted in many areas, including poetry. Thanks to the Beats, poetry has become more spontaneous, energetic, frank and open to common speech. The Beats extended poetry's range primarily through their existence and their evangelical readings and only secondarily through their written poetry. The Beats' accomplishment through life-style rather than on the printed page raises another basic question: can we measure a poet by his intentions and the amount of social change his example causes or must the final assessment rest on the poems themselves, which will be read after the poet and his age have passed? Both friends and foes of the Beats have judged them according to their life-style. Yet after more than twenty years the Beat style of writing has ossified and its mannerisms have inhibited some younger poets. While admiring the Beats' bold attempt to prophesy to America, I have attempted to restore the balance by considering the merits of poems rather than poets.

the Razor's Edge":
The Extremists

Think of a horrifying car crash. Try to focus your memory or imagination not on the injured or on the twisted metal but on the bystanders' various responses: one person, sickened by the sight of blood, will rush away; another, upset by the victim's moans, will hold his hand and try to comfort him; yet a third person, although compassionate, will calmly clear the victim's air passages and stop his bleeding. It is this third type of person, sympathetic yet able to assess the situation, whom the reader must become in order to judge the Extremist poets. The subjects of their poems are often harrowing mental breakdowns, suicides and deaths. In addition, what is widely known about their lives may move us to pity. However, as we have seen with the Beats, lives are not poems, and we should not judge poems more favorably because we feel sorry for the poets.

But don't poems that shock intensify our awareness and so fulfill our criterion? Not necessarily: for intensified awareness means that we understand more as well as feel more. Shock also diminishes on repeated readings, whereas a poem that intensifies our awareness should retain and even increase its effect each time we read it. And it must be our awareness that is widened: a poem must awaken us to what is within ourselves. In Lowell's picture of a madhouse he warns us "We are all old-timers, / Each of us holds a locked razor."[1] The reader must separate the Extremist poets' actual lives from the *personae* which they created in their poems. This is difficult, because these poets deliberately used their own very particular feelings as metaphors for wider meanings. At their strongest, Extremist poets carved their own lives into grotesque but potent images which shaped intense individual suffering into concentrated images of universal tragedy.

M. L. Rosenthal has called this group of poets "Confessional" and A. Alvarez has called them "Extremist." Both labels have their limitations, but they are a convenient shorthand for the intense exploration of the limits of inner feeling and sanity which characterizes the work of Robert Lowell, Sylvia Plath, W. D. Snodgrass, John Berryman and Anne Sexton. Emotionally, they are like the dangerously straying husband Lowell describes "freelancing out along the razor's edge. . . ."[2] Despite their common subject matter, there are important differences among these Extremist poets, which will become apparent as we discuss them.

The appearance of Robert Lowell's *Life Studies* in 1959 was a pivotal point not only for Lowell, but for poetry in general. Lowell's earlier poems had been intricate, symbolic, lush with myths and allusions: a happy hunting ground for the New Critics. *Life Studies* was as direct as the shadowless light above a surgeon's operating table. Lowell not only dissected his own mental turmoil more frankly than his contemporaries had done, and found a style that was as raw as his experience, but he shaped that experience so it could be widely felt. He also helped to make acceptable the open revelation of a poet's own emotional upheaval. No longer did poets have to stand in the impersonal "middle distance" of the fifties academic poets, nor were poets forced to assume the heroic stance of the forties war poets. Lowell intended *Life Studies* to set poetry free: ". . . it seems to me we've gotten into a sort of Alexandrian Age. Poets of my generation and particularly younger ones have gotten terribly proficient at these forms. They write a very musical, difficult poem with tremendous skill. Yet the writing seems divorced from culture somehow. It's become too much something specialized that can't handle much experience. It's become a craft, purely a craft, and there must be some breakthrough back into life."[3]

Robert Lowell both represented and suffered from a uniquely

American dilemma: the Tradition of Rebellion. Even when he sought to escape his ancestors by rebelling against them, his very rebellion identified him with his forebears, who had rebelled against the Church of England, founded the New England colonies and thrown off the sovereignty of Britain. Whether he rebelled or conformed he could not escape his tribal spirits. These clashing rocks of rebellion and tradition, Lowell's Scylla and Charybdis, send waves of tension and ambivalence throughout his entire work. This tension was good for his poetry, but devastating to his person; Lowell had to be hospitalized for numerous nervous breakdowns. The reader who seeks Robert Lowell on the library shelves must first pass a hefty stack of books by his cousin, the redoubtable Amy Lowell, and rows and rows of gold-embossed volumes by James Russell Lowell, Robert's great-grand-uncle. Not only were his ancestors illustrious in politics, but they were famous poets, which might have daunted the young Lowell. Yet he never ceased rebelling and returning: he left Harvard (with which his family was historically connected) after his first year to study with John Crowe Ransome at Kenyon College; here he came under the influence of Allen Tate and the southern *Fugitive* group. In 1940 Lowell converted to Roman Catholicism, and its imagery hangs heavily over his early poems. This was not only a spiritual rebellion against his family but also a social rebellion: Catholicism was the religion of the *parvenu* Irish and Italians who were beginning to contest the old settlers' families who had dominated Boston. "Still, even in the palmy, laissez-faire '20s, Revere Street refused to be a straightforward, immutable residential fact. From one end to the other, houses kept being sanded down, repainted, or abandoned to the flaking of decay. Houses, changing hands, changed their language and nationality. . . . My mother felt a horrified giddiness about the adventure of our address. She once said, 'We are barely perched on the outer rim of the hub of decency.' "[4] Lowell replaced the hierarchy of his family with the even more stringent hierarchy of the Catholic Church, and after a few years renounced that also. In World War II Lowell tried to enlist (his father had been a naval commander with an unremarkable career); when he was rejected on medical grounds, he became "a fire-breathing CO" in protest at the bombing of Dresden and spent five months in jail, which he described in "Memories of West Street and Lepke." In 1946 Lowell's second book of poems, *Lord Weary's Castle*, won the Pulitzer Prize and he was rapidly acclaimed as the leading poet of his day. Yet his "Tradition of Rebellion" would not let him live meekly under any authority, even his own, and his style was always changing. In the Kennedy era, Lowell had visited the White House; when Lyndon Johnson invited him to a "Festival of the Arts" in 1965, Lowell refused to go and publicly condemned the Vietnam war. Even in *Life Studies*, which frankly depicted his parents' weaknesses and failures, there is a nostalgic, elegiac tone, and he was unable to write as bluntly as he did about them until after they died in the fifties. In Lowell, the opposites of tradition and rebellion were yoked like the negative and positive poles of a generator, and produced immense energy.

Although Lowell's poetry appears to undergo dramatic changes, these shifts are part of the continuous crackling movement of tension between contraries. Lowell tenaciously and radically revised and republished his poems, particularly in his later years. Poems from *Notebook*, for example, were reworked as *For Lizzie and Harriet*. The poems that followed *Life Studies* were not written at its fever pitch and were more conventional in form; yet Lowell never allowed his fame to substitute for skill and persisted in redrafting any poems which did not completely satisfy him.

It might be argued that, in undergoing apparently drastic changes that are actually the continuing growth of a tradition, Lowell's work is a microcosm of recent poetry, whose radical changes and challenges are actually current flowerings of older traditions. The Academics followed Eliot and Stevens, the Black Mountain poets are the natural heirs of Pound, and the Beats' forebears were Whitman and Crane. These are some of the boundaries which exist even "out of bounds." The Tradition of Rebellion and the tension associated with it thus apply not only to Lowell but are a widespread force in recent American poetry.

One of Lowell's major accomplishments is to encapsulate many struggles of past and contemporary political history within the version of his own life which his poems present.

> Recuperating, I neither spin nor toil.
> Three stories down below,
> a choreman tends our coffin's length of soil,
> and seven horizontal tulips blow.
> Just twelve months ago,

> these flowers were pedigreed
> imported Dutchmen, now no one need
> distinguish them from weed.
> Bushed by the late spring snow,
> they cannot meet
> another year's snowballing enervation.
>
> I keep no rank nor station.
> Cured, I am frizzled, stale and small.[5]

Like the tulips, Lowell's family were once "pedigreed imports" but "now no one need distinguish them from weed." Not only were Lowell's family unable to cope with the harsh blasts of the twentieth century, but he himself has wilted: "Cured, I am frizzled, stale and small." This is a result of the chemical truncheons used to subdue him in the mental hospital, and of the decade itself, which in the next poem he calls "the tranquillized *Fifties*." McCarthyism and cultural conformity were also the freezing winds of "another year's snowballing enervation." Here, as in many of his poems, Lowell's genius for combining autobiography and history in a form that transcends both to become a personal myth enables him to write poems that are epic (even if unheroic) in a classical yet contemporary manner. Sometimes Lowell seems to regard the past as a lost golden age, particularly when he writes about his grandparents:

> They're altogether otherworldly now. . . .
> the Pierce Arrow clears its throat in a horse-stall. . . .
> the nineteenth century, tired of children, is gone.
> They're all gone into a world of light; the farm's my own.
>
> Grandpa! Have me, hold me, cherish me!
> Tears smut my fingers. There
> half my life-lease later,
> I hold an *Illustrated London News*,
> disloyal still,
> I doodle handlebar
> mustaches on the last Russian Czar.[6]

As always, Lowell is ambivalent, particularly toward his more distant forebears. The contrast of the present (often as represented by Lowell's parents) with the splendors and terrors of the past results in an atmosphere of decline that overshadows many of Lowell's poems. This theme, that grand traditions have now come to ignominious ends, is also used by a number of other twentieth-century poets, notably Eliot and Pound.

Lowell's life was ruled by the strenuous moral and aesthetic demands he made upon himself: just as his forebears in the Massachusetts Bay Colony had been ruled by the rigid requirements of their theocracy. When Lowell converted to Catholicism, he was fascinated by St. Augustine, whose major work, *The City of God*, depicts a divine kingdom governed by heavenly laws. The Tradition of Rebellion was too strong, however, for Lowell to be subservient for long, even to his own inner dictates; and this may have been one factor in his repeated breakdowns. Lowell's immense intelligence and artistry sometimes lacked a steady hand on the tiller, even as the gargantuan power of the United States in the later decades of Lowell's life was sometimes controlled by eccentric, isolated and deeply disturbed men.

Lowell portrays his own mental breakdowns without flinching or self-pity. In "Man and Wife" he and his wife, after a heated quarrel, lie tranquilized but sleepless at dawn on his mother's bed.[7] Lowell conveys this complex scene with courage and skill. His use of detail is sharp and relentless: "*Miltown*," "Marlborough Street," "the Rahvs." The strength of this poem also comes from its open articulation of the forbidden: just as the terror of emotional disturbance can arise from its removal of the polite blinkers that enable us to plod half-blind through normal life. As Lowell said, recalling his stay in a mental hospital in "Waking in the Blue": "Azure day / makes my agonized blue window bleaker."[8] Lowell's raw revelations are contained within intricate yet unobtrusive constructions of rhyme and meter. "Man and Wife," for instance, contains eight end rhymes in its first part; these cease in the second section, which describes his wife's anger (this last section is held together by several internal rhymes). One of the hallmarks of Lowell's poetry is his subtle distribution of images throughout a poem, such as, in "Man and Wife," those for heat and fervor ("sun," "war paint," "red," "ignite," "heat," "boiled," "scorched",) those for loss of reason, unbalance ("abandoned," "Dionysian," "murderous," "mad," "homicidal," "heart in mouth," "outdrank," "fainting," "boiled") and those that echo his childhood ("Mother's bed," "held your hand," "dragged me home," "*Petite*," "in your twenties," "traditional," "like a child," "old-fashioned," "Atlantic Ocean"). Lowell's gift is evident when the images that represent several themes coincide in one word, such as "boiled," which not only means heated to its highest point, but is slang for dead drunk. The cross-weaving of distinct but often slightly bizarre images is similar to the work of dreams as they juggle memories, impulses and events into a pattern that is not too painful to enter consciousness. Also similar to dreams are Lowell's adroit shifts of time and place. In "Man and Wife" he shuttles back twelve years to the night he first met his wife in Greenwich Village and then returns to the present in Boston. These shifts of images, time and place, and style also reflect Lowell's basic ambivalence, the Tradition of Rebellion, which infuses all his work. The magnolia blossoms, although long awaited, are "murderous" white; his wife's tirade is simultaneously "loving, rapid, merciless"; and the Atlantic Ocean is both cooling and drowning.

Despite the horrors and pressures of his time and his calling, Lowell survived; and not only survived his stress but transformed it in his poetry. In "My Last Afternoon with Uncle Devereaux Winslow," Lowell recalls the tension at his grandfather's farm while Devereaux was dying of incurable Hodgkin's disease at twenty-nine: "I cowered in terror. / I wasn't a child at all— / unseen and all-seeing, I was Agrippina / in the Golden House of Nero. . . ."[9] Lowell never glamorized his bouts of mental breakdown, as became trendy in the late sixties (although he could be witty about the absurdities of the mental hospital). "I have been through both mania and depression; *Life Studies* is about neither. Mania is extremity for one's friends, depression for one's self. . . . I don't think it is a visitation of the angels but dust in the blood."[10] These qualities of survival and his enormous gift and skill place Lowell not only beyond the other Extremist poets, but in the front rank of all modern poets. In 1977, while traveling in a cab from Kennedy Airport into Manhattan, he had a fatal heart attack. This was too early a death, but a doubly "natural" one: for it was Lowell who had made the sharpest "attack of the heart" on a poetry that had become as cold as New England granite tombstones.

Many people who have not read Sylvia Plath's poetry have heard that her husband, Ted Hughes, left her with two very small children, that she wrote emotionally abrasive poems and that she killed herself. This information makes it difficult to view her poems purely as literature. She also made herself vulnerable to back-seat psychiatrists by so frankly exposing the dark side of her mind in her poetry. In addition she has been used for propaganda by both poetic suicide fans and by certain feminists, who parade her as a classic example of A-Poor-Brilliant-Woman-Driven-Into-Her-Grave-By-Domestic-Woes. It is important to remember that Plath's most candid book, *Ariel*, although her last, was not intended to be her *final* work (at the time she wrote to her mother of plans for more novels and poetry), but was written in only one of the many tones with which she experimented throughout her life. Often readers will look at the poems in *Ariel* and project their themes backwards into her earlier books; we should try to think of the poems she wrote up to age thirty-one as moving forward, like the curve of an unfinished archway, and even try to outline what directions her later work might have taken.

The problem of disentangling Plath's life, her imagination and her art become apparent when we look at poems such as "Ariel." At the time when she was writing it, Sylvia Plath had become more skilled at poetry but more careless about her physical safety. Or perhaps the rigid self-discipline necessary for her to continue writing and the constant concern for the security of her small children made her feel a need to be reckless for a change. She had always enjoyed taking risks, such as skiing down an advanced slope before she had really learned to ski, and in late summer 1962 she drove her car off a country road in an attempt to kill herself. Ted Hughes in a note to "Ariel" says the poem arose partly from an incident when they were students at Cambridge while she was out riding (before having taken lessons). Her horse bolted and she had to cling to its neck for two miles at full gallop.[11] Several years later, when Sylvia Plath first showed "Ariel" to A. Alvarez, she left him with the impression that she was teaching herself to ride on a powerful stallion called Ariel. (It is unheard of for stallions to be used as beginners' mounts, because of their strength and temperament; Ariel was probably a gelding.) In fact, at this time Sylvia Plath had been building her equestrian skills as methodically as she had built her poetic skills: she wrote her mother that she had been taking weekly lessons from a qualified instructor.[12] Nor is the poem "Ariel" accurate as a literal description of what it feels like to be on a runaway horse—the rider is terrified because he has *lost* contact with the rhythm of the horse's motion and at any second may be "at one" with the blurred ground below. But all these discrepancies with literal fact do not mean that "Ariel" is not a compelling poem; on the contrary, its strength is that the Ariel of the poem is not the headstrong horse at Cambridge, nor the stallion she claimed she was learning to master herself, nor the riding-school gelding, but an imaginary beast she created, just as the mythical winged horse, Pegasus, who symbolized poetry, sprang from Medusa's blood. Because "Ariel" is an imaginary horse, he is able to bear a number of complex and contradictory meanings. When we speak of "Sylvia Plath," we must always be quite certain to draw clear bounds among the *persona* she created in her poetry, the actual woman and her interior fantasies about herself. That she herself could not always distinguish among literature, physical reality and her imagination gave moments of breathtaking force to her poetry, but was partly the cause of so much pain that finally she ended her life and her poetry.

The conventional view is that Sylvia Plath's poems are literal and frank self-revelations. But when we set aside our store of biographical details, we are surprised to discover how many of her poems are concerned with concealment and obscurity. This is particularly true of the poems she wrote about bees, which culminated in a sustained sequence in *Ariel*. Often the characters in these poems are not only featureless but those literally veiled, such as beekeepers, a masking that continues with other subjects in other poems. The villagers who are transferring the bees in "The Bee Meeting" are covered in veils, protective suits and gloves, and their identity is questioned at the opening of the poem: "Who are these people at the bridge to meet me?" [13] Even the identities proposed for the villagers are abstract roles rather than faces: "the butcher," "the grocer," rather than "Mr. Tucker" or "our red-faced butcher with the blue-striped apron." This veiling of the subject adds great mystery and possibility to what are, on the surface, straightforward factual descriptions. The narrator is passive and vulnerable: "I am exhausted, I am exhausted— / Pillar of white in a blackout of knives." [14] Not only is the speaker stone-like, but she often merges with her surroundings. Sometimes Plath's narrator even melts through the barriers that would normally have separated her self from the world and her fears; just as a tiny infant has not yet formed boundaries of "me" and "not me."

Although Plath's bee poems could have been a series of set pieces, careful sketches, they vibrate with a tension, a potential sting. And with good reason: for although this sequence is ostensibly about bees, it is haunted by the gray veiled figure of Sylvia Plath's father, renowned authority on bees, whose childhood nickname was "the bee king" and whose death when she was eight shattered her childhood. "Hieratical in your frock coat, maestro of the bees, / you move among the many breasted hives." [15] This is the father readers will remember her denouncing in her vitrolic poem "Daddy." There may also be oblique references to her father in other bee poems: "someone I know?" in "The Bee Meeting"; in "The Swarm," "The man with grey hands smiles— / The smile of a man of business, intensely practical. / They are not hands at all / But asbestos receptacles." [16] The strange figure in the eighth stanza of "Stings" may well be her father, who wrote a book on bees, yet ironically died from diabetes, a surfeit of sweetness, which is what honeybees produce. (His diabetes was not diagnosed until it was far advanced, because he had refused to consult doctors despite his failing health—a kind of suicide.) "The sweat of his efforts a rain / Tugging the world to fruit. / The bees found him out, / Moulding onto his lips like lies, / Complicating his features." [17] Plath can handle explosive subjects such as her father in veiled forms and yet reveal their full power at the reader's most vulnerable moment.

If a poet is lucky, after years of careful poems or experimental poems or both, there may come a sudden release of mature talent— Robert Duncan calls this "permission." Sylvia Plath's book *Ariel* represents a freedom from her previous concern about literary safety, just as she was now becoming less concerned about physical safety. A. Alvarez (who has written a perceptive yet compassionate biography of Plath in *The Savage God*) noticed not only a new confidence but also a sharpness and clarity about her when he visited her in Devon at this time. The poems in her earlier books had been highly polished and competent, rather in the style of Auden and Roethke. The new poems in *Ariel* were powered by sudden intuitions and striking associations rather than tidy artifices. Her bold and angry wit broke through the previously sedate tone of her poems. Here there is a struggle to reveal identities, a progressive baring not only of her emotions but more significantly of those veiled figures. "Only let down the veil, the veil." [18] Her former passive merging into nature has now become a protean grasping of her environment and re-creation of it in her image; she metamorphoses herself into an icon, into a red queen bee. It is this transforming power, both of her subject and of her own emotions, that makes the *Ariel* poems so effective. Had her work been allowed to continue, she may well have moved even further beyond autobiography into art.

Like Ariel, and many other images in her poems, death and suicide cannot be understood by their literal value alone, however tempting it is to read them in the light of Plath's actual suicide. Not only has she conflicting dread of and erotic desire for death and her dead father, but death itself has many faces as she portrays it in "Death and Co." What appears to be death may be a larval stage, like the caddis worms she writes about: "This is not death, it is something safer. / The wingy myths won't tug at us anymore." [19] By the time of the Ariel poems her elaborate concealments of death had themselves become a kind of death, literary and emotional. "If only you knew how the veils were killing my days, / To you they are only transparencies, clean air. / But my god the clouds are like cotton. / Armies of them. They are carbon monoxide." [20] The veils that had protected her from the angry bees and from the sight of her dead father have become a suffocating cloud of poisonous gas.

Gas, of course, is what Plath used to kill herself and brings us to the biographical aspect of her poems. Yet the "facts" about Sylvia Plath are more complicated than the popular version. First, all the other principals in the drama are still alive; while it is an advantage to have their opinions of events, Plath's relations with other people were far from simple and sometimes in conflict, and biographers have been wary of the sensibilities of the living and of the strict British libel laws. Sylvia Plath's suicide (like the images in her poems) was more complex than a simple wish to end her own life. A. Alvarez has made a convincing case that her suicide was a gesture, a cry for help which she could not make in any other way. It is logical that she would be reluctant to seek psychiatric help, even if she were desperate, since her first suicide attempt ten years previously had been "treated" (or punished) not only with insulin (which would have saved her father) but with electroconvulsive shocks, which frequently obscure the patient's memory and intellect, two vital elements of a poet's being and art. Alvarez also suggests that she could write so candidly about suicide because she had survived her attempt ten years previously and had moved beyond that stage in her life.

In the light of these facts, the effusions of the sensational suicidal poetic martyr cult are exceptionally silly and superficial: ". . . the

very source of Sylvia Plath's creative energy was her self-destruc-
tiveness."[21] "Plath was lonely and isolated. Her genius did not earn
for her certain reprieves and comforts tendered the male artist. No
one, and especially men of culture, felt 'responsible' for her plight or
felt responsible to honor the poet by 'saving' the woman."[22] This last
comment, in addition to being quaintly medieval in its concept of Sylvia Plath as a damsel in distress waiting to be rescued by some literary
knight on a white charger, is quite simply untrue: she wrote her
mother a week before her death that one reason she didn't want to return to the United States was that her career was going so well, with
her poems and novel published, reviewing for national magazines and
work for the BBC, including the prestigious "Critics" program, "a fantastic break I hope I can make good on."[23] Undeniably, Sylvia Plath
had a fascination with death and wrote many bitter and grim, even
pathologically morbid, poems. Yet many of these poems were written
in a comparatively brief period of great personal stress. If a political
prisoner were forced to rise before dawn, labor all day in ill health
while being screeched at and then be jolted awake every few hours
during the night, there would be an international outcry against such
"torture" and "brainwashing." Yet this is the reality of life with tiny
children for millions of women. In addition, the fluctuations of the
female hormones before and after birth can cause such volatile mood
changes that English law has long recognized that no woman can be
held responsible for infanticide (only manslaughter) while pregnant or
for some months afterwards.

Biographical studies of Sylvia Plath can be helpful, but only if they
are kept in proper perspective to her poems. Too much of what has
been written about Sylvia Plath is merely tarted-up tittle-tattle and
plain nosiness rather than attempts to make her difficult poems more
accessible. So often when refering to personal problems in letters to
her mother, Sylvia Plath asked her to keep them private, as they
weren't anyone else's business.

Plath is not content with a simple image that represents one thing
or one feeling, but she fashions dense conglomerates, honey-cell upon
honey-cell, of symbols and metaphors. She begins with an incisive ex-
actness of vision, a possible inheritance from German scientist father.
As she looks into the newly-arrived box of bees: "I put my eye to the
grid. / It is dark, dark, / With the swarmy feeling of African hands /
Minute and shrunk for export, / Black on black, angrily clamber-

ing."[24] When veiled figures do appear in Plath's poems, against such a precisely detailed backdrop, we can be certain that the concealment of these figures is not accidental and that she has loaded them with significance, just as the opaque wax of a brood-cell can conceal a young queen ready to fight her rivals to the death. The same accurate command of fine detail is evident in Sylvia Plath's pen-and-ink drawings, which are as stark as woodcuts.[25] Although conventional, they are well composed and communicate the bulk and mass of the houses and boats which loom toward the viewer. There is a relative lack of shading or cross-hatching in her drawings: surfaces are either solid black or stark white. She used images in her poems in the same way, as palpable symbols. Colors in particular are emotive, and she applied them as boldly as the cut-outs in a Matisse collage. (In her play, *Three Women*, one of her characters speaks of "black, cut-paper people.") Black, white and red are repeated in poem after poem until they accrue highly complex and personal meanings. Red, for instance, appears in the first of the bee poems, "The Beekeeper's Daughter," in a highly sensual description of flowers fertilized by bees: "Scarlet-speckled," "red," "sugar roses."[26] "The Swarm" gives red and its shades a more ominous tone: "Jealousy can open the blood, / It can make black roses"; "the same old magenta / Fields shrunk to a penny"; "A red tatter, Napoleon!"[27] The seductive and menacing aspects of red join in "The Bee Meeting" when the narrator is led through bean flowers: "Is it blood clots the tendrils are dragging up that string? / No, no it is scarlet flowers that will one day be edible."[28] "The barren body of the hawthorn, etherizing its children" in the next stanza bears a pink or white flower and red fruit. In the next poem of the sequence, "The Arrival of the Bee Box," she wonders if she can escape the angry bees by turning into a tree, perhaps a pink-blossomed cherry that bears red fruit, and, later, find contentment with busy-bee housewives: ". . . These women who only scurry, / Whose news is the open cherry, the open clover?"[29] These red and pink images foreshadow the metamorphosis that climaxes "Stings" after the bees have attacked the veiled stranger:

> They thought death was worth it, but I
> Have a self to recover, a queen.
> Is she dead, is she sleeping?
> Where has she been,
> With her lion-red body, her wings of glass?

> Now she is flying
> More terrible than she ever was, red
> Scar in the sky, red comet
> Over the engine that killed her—
> The mausoleum, the wax house.[30]

The last poem in the bee sequence, "Wintering," ends on a positive note, with chords of red images:

> Will the hive survive, will the gladiolas
> Succeed in banking their fires
> To enter another year?
> What will they taste of, the Christmas roses?
> The bees are flying. They taste the spring.[31]

An interesting sidelight to this progressive identification of Plath's strong "queen bee" self with the color red is that her parents had named her Sylvia because they associated it with "sylvan" and with the herb salvia, whose flame-red flowers often persist right into November.[32] This progressive refinement of an image is one of her poetic strengths which probably would have increased in any poems beyond *Ariel*.

Plath's use of "red" is an example of her ability to super-saturate a single word with a multitude of meanings, even contradictory meanings, and to use this conglomerate of metaphor to convey intense and ambivalent inner emotions. These concentrated metaphors, rather than her well-known ability to write about desperate mental states, give her poems their continuing power and fascination.

"Family trouble, troubles in your love life, has caused people a hundred times more real agony than all the wars, famines, oppressions and the other stuff that gets in the history books."[33] The domestic minefield is often W. D. Snodgrass' chosen lode of ore. Like Sylvia Plath, he chronicles the sufferings and anger of family life gone sour, yet his perspective is quite different from hers: not only is he the father who left his wife and child, but he is more ambivalent about his family, perhaps because he is more distant from it. When his first marriage broke up, he was separated from his small daughter, whom he loved very much. When his daughter returned for a visit, they went, as usual, to the zoo:

> If I loved you, they said, I'd leave
> and find my own affairs.
> Well, once again this April, we've
> come around to the bears;
>
> punished and cared for, behind bars,
> the coons on bread and water
> stretch thin black fingers after ours.
> And you are still my daughter. [34]

"Those things that live upon departure understand when you praise them." [35] This line of Rilke's is appropriate for Snodgrass's sequence of poems about his daughter, "Heart's Needle," especially since Snodgrass is a clear and accomplished translator of Rilke. There is an elegiac tone in many of Snodgrass's poems, which often attempt to recapture a lost beloved, as does his Orpheus, "Rich in the loss of all I sing." [36] Snodgrass drove his daughter to the train after another visit:

> Next year we'll hardly know you;
> Still, all the blame endures.
> This year you will live at our expense;
> We have a life at yours. [37]

Yet, like Orpheus (who fatally mistrusted), Snodgrass is himself partly to blame for his beloved's departure. His awareness of his own guilt in causing pain to others and to himself is acute, and adds another dimension not only to his own pain but also to his poems. This leap of his imagination into others' feelings enables him to expose his own emotions forcefully and frankly, yet almost always avoid sentimentality. After years of "cold war" with his ex-wife, he is finally able to say: "[I] though how much grief I'd brought you; / I wished you well again." [38] This same agility of the imagination allows him to handle shocking and grotesque subjects such as "The Platform Man" without hysteria.

> Squat, dark as a troll,
>   with a gripped wooden block
> In each hand, he rolled
>   Himself along the sidewalks

> Or, by the 5 and 10, sat
>   On that wheeled dolly, begging,
> With pencils and a hat
>   Laid on his thick stumps of legs.
>
> His stare leveled with my
>   Stare, when I was a child.
> He felt no need to try
>   Any of those wild
>
> Stunts our tightrope clever
>   Kids do on their cool new boards. . . .
>
> How much could he expect?
>   He wouldn't as much as sing.
> From sideshows, stages, lecterns,
>   We hear men offering
>
> New incredible talents,
>   Spectacular handicaps,
> Who've shaped strange arts to balance
>   Whatever it is they lack.
>
> Some went too far and lost
>   Things he was saved from wanting—
> Influence, love, applause.
>   I'd travel light: take nothing
>
> Free and give no quarter.
>   The curse is far from done
> When they've taken your daughter;
>   They can take your son.[39]

The "curse" in the last stanza is partly a reference to the Middle-Irish romance "The Madness of Suibhne," which provided the title for Snodgrass's first book: " 'Suibhne, your daughter is dead.' 'And an only daughter is a needle of the heart.' 'And Suibhne, your little boy, who used to call you "Daddy"—he is dead.' 'Aye,' said Suibhne, 'that's the drop that brings a man to the ground.' He fell out of the yew tree; Loingseachan closed his arms around him and placed him in manacles."[40] Snodgrass underscores the cripple's grotesqueness by contrasting him with the "clever kids" on their new skateboards who find sport in a wheeled motion which is a painful necessity for the cripple. The beggar is also horrific because he is there "day after day," a familiar small-town specter whose stare levels with the poet's as a child. The jerky rhythms, stumpy lines and constricted rhymes echo the cripple's crabbed movement, as do the breaks between phrases. Although Snodgrass is not an innovator of form, he is adept at choosing a formal pattern which reflects his own concerns and whose demands, such as end rhymes, are unobtrusively met. He is also deft at slipping in puns, such as "troll" and "quarter," that are effective but inconspicuous. By the end of the poem, the "Platform Man" emerges as Snodgrass himself, on lecture and poetry reading platforms. The loss of his daughter is part of a curse which has left him truncated like the amputee, and the poet dreads the loss of his son, his other leg.

There is a circular flow of ideas in this poem which occurs in some of Snodgrass's other poems, whose form may also be circular. As we return to the opening stanzas of "The Platform Man," our realization that the cripple has been a disguise for Snodgrass is strengthened: as a poet, his tools are pencils like those the beggar sells, which are ground down to stumps; on the lecture platform he displays himself for a relatively few pennies. This circling, "trolling" movement is appropriate for Snodgrass's poems even when their subject matter is not as obvious an impasse as it is here in "Heart's Needle": "Three months now we have been apart / less than a mile. I cannot fight / or let you go."[41] Snodgrass once said about this poem: "Plainly, the whole problem of freedom and guilt, which had at first been so very subordinate, must now be developed into a major thematic area, perhaps into the dominant theme."[42]

Although Snodgrass's set forms are superficially similar to those of the academic poets, he uses these forms to expose nerve ends in a way that is quite individual. In one major anthology Snodgrass's biography stated that he had been "deeply influenced by the Texas poet S. S. Gardons."[43] This entry disappeared when the critic Richard Howard, with his lexicographer's training, spotted that "S. S. Gardons" was nothing other than an anagram of "Snodgrass." This hilarious masquerade at the expense of the academy (one imagines earnest graduate students pilgrimaging to Fort Worth and interviewing all the gas station attendants seeking the mythical Gardons) shows that not even a lifetime of university teaching and a Pulitzer Prize can make some poets behave themselves.

Snodgrass and Robert Lowell are often compared, and have had varying influences on each other. But history and politics do not preoccupy Snodgrass as they do Lowell. Like other Extremist poets, Snodgrass explores painful, even anguished emotions; yet while his work is as unremittingly candid as any of the other poets in this group, his conclusions are not melodramatic despair and suicide, but the real necessity of making choices which confronts humans who survive. He remembers a night he sat up with his daughter, who was having an attack of asthma (which had killed his sister):

> Of all things, only we
> have power to choose that we should die;
>   nothing else is free
> in this world to refuse it. Yet I,
>   who say this, could not raise
> myself from bed how many days
> to the thieving world. Child, I have another wife,
>   another child. We try to choose our life.[44]

Although John Berryman began as a rather conventional "academic" poet, he indicated the direction his mature work was taking in "Homage to Mistress Bradstreet" (1956), an imaginary dialogue with the early American poet in which their voices converge and blend as in a seance or dream. Berryman's full attempt to reproduce the dream form is an extremely long series of "Dream Songs" (many written between 1956 and 1968), which is his major work. The landscapes of these poems are the emotions of "Henry," a character Berryman said was not intended to represent himself. Although there is some conversation among Henry, a minstrel show character and Berryman, they are basically one person: other people never really come alive, nor does the natural world. Berryman's flat but fluid world is that of the dream. Berryman quotes with the highest praise a line from his contemporary Delmore Schwartz's *In Dreams Begin Responsibilities*: "The theodicy I wrote in my highschool days / Restored all life from infancy."[45] This is one goal of successful "dream-work." And as Berryman says in Dream Song 271: "Why then did he make, at such cost, *crazy* sounds? / to waken ancient longings, to remind (of childness), / to make laugh, and to hurt, / is and was all he ever intended. . . ."[46] But he takes issue with the idea (which he mistakenly attributes to Freud) that dreams are *only* a transcript of childhood and insists that "a dream is a panorama / of the whole mental life. . . ."[47]

In an attempt to reproduce dreams, *Dream Songs* sprawls with talk, memories and urges in a "stream-of-consciousness" style. Words are abruptly shunted into an arbitrary order. Although each poem in *Dream Songs* has its own form (eighteen lines per poem, but various schemes of end rhymes), their weak verbs and hazy subject-matter make them sag as one reads page after page of similar poems. The chatty, casual poem has had a long history in America, and Berryman said his Dream Songs were modeled on *Song of Myself*. But Berryman lacks Whitman's energy and scope. Rather than revise poems he was dissatisfied with, Berryman would often write another poem on the same subject and publish both (see Dream Songs 154 and 155, for example).

After a number of Dream Songs many readers will pull up sharply and ask, "Just what *exactly* is this man complaining about?" There are inarticulate grumbles in the early Dream Songs, rather like a toddler who is crying so hard he cannot say where he is hurt. "Huffy Henry hid the day / unappeasable Henry sulked. / I see his point,—a trying to put things over. / It was the thought that they thought / they could *do* it made Henry wicked & away. / But he should have come out and talked."[48] Not until Dream Song 76, "Henry's Confession," do we learn that Berryman's father shot himself. Part of the "dream-work" that has to be accomplished, then, is a coming to terms with various deaths: the father's suicide, deaths of friends—especially Delmore Schwartz's—and the narrator's own impulses toward suicide. Often there is a lack of vitality and development in *Dream Songs*: this "deadlock" is the grip of the well-loved dead who paralyze the narrator through identification and guilt. He is tempted to join them so he will be "not guilty by reason of death."[49] Berryman has said that "the artist is extremely lucky who is presented with the worst possible ordeal which will not actually kill him."[50] Berryman records his various ordeals: his father's suicide, his own broken marriages and his mental breakdowns:

> It seems to be DARK all the time.
> I have difficulty walking.
> I can remember what to say to my seminar
> but I don't know that I want to.

I said in a Song once: I am unusually tired.
I repeat that & increase it.
I'm vomiting.
I broke down today in the slow movement of K.365.[51]

Because much of Berryman's poetry is so self-centered and does not reach out to others, it is difficult for the reader to feel compassion for his woes, which are not all that unique.

With Berryman we are faced once again with the problem of *persona*: the personality a poet projects to his readers. Indeed, *persona*, not new verse forms and techniques, has become a central problem for post-Modernist poets, and we have already seen the difficulties which Larkin's and Ginsberg's *personae* can present. Like the early heroes of his friend, Saul Bellow, Berryman's *persona* in *Dream Songs* is anti-heroic: "We dream of honour, and we get along."[52] This tone leads to odd mixtures of formality and slang: "Whence flew the litter whereon he was laid? / Of what heroic stuff was warlock Henry made? / and questions of that sort / perplexed the bulging cosmos. . . ."[53] Berryman sometimes breaks into minstrel show dialect in *Dream Songs*. Although this "blacking up" may have given him a certain risqué thrill in the civil rights years, it is shallow, somewhat offensive, and shoddily done. Even his associations between the raccoon hunted and treed by dogs and the "coon" of the stage are obvious and ineffective. But the most serious difficulty with Berryman's *persona* is that it gets in the way, like a thumb held over the lens by an amateur photographer. "Henry" never develops into a fully independent character because Berryman keeps interrupting him and breaking any imaginative spell between "Henry" and the reader. Berryman keeps waking us from the dream he is trying to induce. Anyone who has ever been handed a book of poems to read whose author then kept flipping the pages to show off more poems before one could finish reading the first will have a similar sense of irritation and awkwardness when reading Berryman, who continually intrudes to remind us that he is writing a poem, he is miserable, he is famous, he has girlfriends, he knows famous poets, etc., etc.

Berryman's huge reputation seems to have been based partly on the sheer quantity of his output, his friendships and perhaps his knack for filling the role expected of a poet in America, particularly an "Extremist": he had several marriages, affairs, a drinking problem, stints in a mental hospital, and he finally killed himself in 1972 by jumping from a bridge.

Although Berryman's work is uneven and erratic, at certain moments he is able to articulate an overwhelming despair which most poets are unable to write, or even talk, about. Some of his strongest poems are those about the mental hospital in *Love and Fame* and one of the final Dream Songs:

> The marker slants, flowerless, day's almost done,
> I stand above my father's grave with rage,
> often, often before
> I've made this awful pilgrimage to one
> who cannot visit me, who tore his page
> out: I come back for more,
>
> I spit upon this dreadful banker's grave
> who shot his heart out in a Florida dawn
> O ho alas alas
> When will indifference come, I moan & rave
> I'd like to scrabble till I got right down
> away down under the grass
>
> and ax the casket open ha to see
> just how he's taking it, which he sought so hard
> we'll tear apart
> the mouldering grave clothes ha & then Henry
> will heft the ax once more, his final card,
> and fell it on the start.[54]

Was it necessary for these Extremist poets to have undergone crises, nervous breakdowns and even suicide for their poetry to be authentic? Is it necessary to know of the Aztecs' vast sacrificial murders to feel a chill when looking down those bottomless eyesockets of crystal in the skull they made? No: for it is the object or the poem itself that intensifies our artistic awareness, not details of the poet's life, although these may make us feel pity or admiration. While the Extremists wrote vivid poetry about desperate emotional situations, these same crises so interfered in their lives that writing poetry became difficult, and after suicide, obviously impossible. Going out of bounds emotionally may have been a necessary risk, both for the Extremist poets and for poetry in general after the formalist fifties. But the best Extremist poets held onto enough artistic sanity to construct a *persona*, a crystal skull, with which they could relate to readers. Madness and suffering alone are not enough: they only reinforce the image of the crazy bohemian self-destructive poet which is so imbedded in Middle America, where "the only good poet is a dead one."

6

"Neon in Daylight":
The New York Poets

Frank O'Hara, the most "New York" of all the New York poets, wrote, "It's my lunch hour, so I go / for a walk among the hum-colored cabs. . . . / Neon in daylight is a / great pleasure. . . ."[1] And when you visit New York, you are likely to arrive from the airport in a typical New York taxi: one of thousands that rattle through the streets like battered yellow armadillos. Although these cabs are similar and serve the same purpose, each of their drivers is highly idiosyncratic and may tell you his life story, or stare sullenly in the mirror, or cross-examine you like an anxious granny. Even if you ask for the same address each driver may take you there by a different route, and you will encounter diverse traffic on the way. So it is with the New York poets: although they share an urban environment, each is so distinct that many people (including some of the New York poets) question whether they can be regarded as a group at all. Yet they are friends and collaborators, are frequently published in the same magazines and have left a collective mark on a second generation. In addition to this (and New York City) these poets share three common ideas which shaped their work.

The first of these concepts is Surrealism. As we have seen, younger poets in the fifties were confronted by the paramount influence of Eliot and the New Critics. The academic poets accepted this and wrote in forms and about subjects which could be understood within the limits set by the New Critics. Fortified by Olson's theory of Projective Verse, the Black Mountain poets attempted to write "open verse." The Beat poets rebelled not only against the New Critics, but against criticism itself, and their life-style and poetry were bohemian and neo-Romantic. The Extremist poets wrote about emotional states that had been off-limits for the genteel academic poets. The New York poets also rejected establishment literary criticism; but instead they applied certain canons of *art* criticism to their poetry. Most of these poets earned their livings as art critics, which meant that (despite occasional lip-service paid to Surrealist anti-art and anti-rational attitudes) they were accustomed to looking at works of art and to writing with strong visual imagery. Although "surreal" has acquired the wider meanings of "irrational" and "dream-like," when Apollinaire first used the term he was describing an attempt to reproduce in art the processes of the unconscious mind. André Breton, whose *Surrealist manifestos* codified the movement from 1924 onward, used "automatic writing" as the criterion to judge if a work was surrealist or not.[2] Automatic writing is the aspect of Surrealism most relevant to the New York poets, whose poems often appear to have the same illogical juxtapositions of subject matter as dreams. These poets used surrealist techniques as what John Ashbery called "an expanded means of utterance," one of several devices for "getting into remoter areas of consciousness."[3] This is part of the "widening of awareness" which many poets and others were seeking in the sixties and which we have set as a criterion for poetry.

The second concept which characterized the New York poets is the importance of the Present Moment. Just as dreams often seem to take place in an enormous present time, so the poems of the New York poets were concerned with what was happening in the immediate moment. History on a grand scale and myths were ignored, except for the mock-epics of Koch and Ashbery's dream landscapes, both of which are too private to be universal myths. "It's time to write one of my 'I do this, I do that' poems," said Frank O'Hara.[4] Present actions preoccupied the New York poets, just as the action painters (whom the poets knew and wrote about) used automatic painting to reach the unconscious. The New York poets' emphasis on the present means that their poems are not intensely detailed studies in perspective but that they are wide rather than intense, like the large fields of flat color painted by some Abstract Expressionists. Certain New York poems seem to be "abstract" in the sense that they lack one definite subject or narrative sequence. Their flow of ideas and images does not stop long enough for us to see the outlines of the poets' personalities behind them; the poets themselves are abstract.

The third concept which the New York poets shared is the importance of the Ordinary: everyday events and speech. This may seem paradoxical, since these poets were attracted to Surrealist ideas, but after some early flings with French imitations, most settled into the colloquial diction and concern with common events that was typical of American poets such as Whitman and Williams. "We are in America and it is all right not to be elsewhere," affirmed Frank O'Hara.[5]

When reading the New York poets it helps to keep in mind these three shared concepts which led to such diverse results and to read in a casual manner, with our critical guard temporarily down. Many New York poems do not disclose the secret of their charm through close repeated readings or the laborious teasing out of every in-group reference any more than do those Japanese paper flowers which seem so marvelous when they open under water but become a sodden wad of tissue if we try to dissect them. (An exception must be made for certain of John Ashbery's complex poems, which reward close reading.) But, if the New York poets are granted this relaxed acceptance, the reader must demand in return that the poems be effective on the very first reading. Many New York poems will not stand the stress of repeated readings because they were written to capture a moment or a mood rather than make grand philosophical statements. The reader must also be prepared to find that the conventional signposts that guide him or her into a poem—such as "what is this about?" and "what happens next?"—have been stolen or spray-painted with nonsense.

This method of reading the New York poets (relaxed, but requiring an instant response) is particularly useful for the poems of Frank O'Hara. A gifted pianist (influenced by John Cage), he first majored in music at Harvard, where he met John Ashbery and others who were to remain lifelong friends. They founded the Poets' Theater in Cambridge and made trips to New York, where O'Hara soon made contact

with the poet Kenneth Koch and with Larry Rivers and other Abstract
Expressionist painters who were launching their assault on the art establishment.

> We were all in our early twenties. John Ashbery, Barbara
> Guest, Kenneth Koch and I, being poets, divided our time
> between the literary bar, the San Remo, and the artists' bar,
> the Cedar Tavern. In the San Remo we argued and gossiped:
> in the Cedar we often wrote poems while listening to the
> painters argue and gossip. So far as I know nobody painted in
> the San Remo while they listened to the writers argue. An
> interesting sidelight to these social activities was that for most
> of us non-Academic and indeed non-literary poets in the
> sense of the American scene at that time, the painters were
> the only generous audience for our poetry, and most of us
> first read publicly in art galleries or at The Club.[6]

A few years after he had begun to write poetry, O'Hara stated that
his method was surprise:

> The only way to be quiet
> is to be quick, so I scare
> you clumsily, or surprise
> you with a stab. . . .
>   To
> deepen you by my quickness
> and delight as if you
> were logical and proven,
> but still be quiet as if
> I were used to you; as if
> you would never leave me
> and were the inexorable
> product of my own time.[7]

Surrealism is O'Hara's tactic for surprising the reader so he is
"deepened" and "delighted." When O'Hara's scrap heaps of surreal
images, like Jean Tinguely's "junk machines," manage to move grace-
fully, they not only startle us but please us by avoiding obvious desti-
nations. O'Hara is sometimes belligerent, a tiger pissing in a porcelain

teapot, but this tone conceals a very squashy center indeed. Not all of
his poems are long and surreal: some of his very best poems are short,
intense love lyrics addressed very much to a particular person at a particular time (an enormous Present Moment) but with a clarity and
conviction that involve a wider readership and other times. O'Hara's
particular safari out of bounds is into a lush jungle of sentiment: sometimes the creepers entangle him, but at other times he returns with exotic and beautiful orchids.

> . . . One of [Personism's] minimal aspects is to address one-
> self to one person (other than the poet himself), thus evoking
> overtones of love without destroying love's life-giving vulgar-
> ity, and sustaining the poet's feeling about the person. That's
> part of Personism. It was founded by me after lunch with Le
> Roi Jones on August 27th 1959, a day in which I was in love
> with someone (not Roi, by the way, a blond). I went back to
> work and wrote a poem for this person. While I was writing it
> I was realizing that if I wanted to I could use the telephone
> instead of writing the poem, and so Personism was born.[8]

This is the core of O'Hara's "Personism: A Manifesto" (much of which
is a parody of the deadly earnest art critical "isms" of that time). Although there is nothing radically new here (the Provençal poets and
the tradition of courtly love are precedents), it is this "personal" element which acts as a catalyst for random assemblies in O'Hara's poetry
and makes them cohere, as does the lover's presence in:

> Light   clarity   avocado salad in the morning
> after all the terrible things I do how amazing it is
> to find forgiveness and love, not even forgiveness. . . .
> though a block away you feel distant the mere presence
> changes everything like a chemical dropped on a paper
> and all thoughts disappear in a strange quiet excitement
> I am sure of nothing but this, intensified by breathing[9]

The Ordinary, which provides so much of O'Hara's material, is given
an intensified dimension by his lover's presence.
    O'Hara was not content with sentiment alone: he ventured his ten-
derest feelings and fantasies against one of the harshest realities man

has ever constructed—New York City. This is one of many pairs of opposites in O'Hara's poetry: city vs. country, artifice vs. nature. Yoked together, these opposites balance each other: sentiment doesn't become gooey, realism doesn't become cold and uncaring. Naturally, given the vast number of poems O'Hara wrote, this balance doesn't work one hundred per cent of the time, but it succeeds in his best poems.

One of these contradictions is the sterile vs. the fecund, homosexuality vs. "nature." Homosexuality becomes associated with the concrete and metal of New York City which do not reproduce themselves, although they are a crucible for human encounters and imaginative endeavor. O'Hara not only came to terms with his sexual orientation but celebrated it in lyrics and exuberant verses such as "At the Old Place": "Jack, Earl and Someone drift / guiltily in. 'I knew they were gay / the minute I laid eyes on them!' screams John. / How ashamed they are of us! we hope."[10] Sometimes he briefly wonders if such a relationship (and the city which makes it possible) is barren, and imagines having a son to carry on his "staggering load": "he lifts a little of the load each day /as I become more and more idiotic / and grows to be a strong strong man / and one day carries as I die / my final idiocy and the very gates / into a future of his choice. . . ."[11]

The link that chains together these opposites is the same that ordered O'Hara's surreal images: a particular person. His poems are "a great city / I was building to house the myth of my love."[12] Because New York is the watering-place for those he loves, the city becomes more rich and "pastoral" than the countryside. "One need never leave the confines of New York to get all the greenery one wishes—I can't even enjoy a blade of grass unless I know there's a subway handy, or a record store or some other sign that people do not totally *regret* life."[13] O'Hara accepts the hard, man-made city because it contains person(s) he loves. Yet O'Hara's love and imagination transform the artificial city into a natural landscape, into a "sur-real," "super-natural" "myth of love." By creating this lush and fantastic yet apparently real New York, O'Hara succeeded at urban romanticism when most of his contemporaries failed.

> I am out of context waiting
> for the place where my life exists like a tree
> in a meadow

> the warm traffic going by is my natural scenery
> because I am not alone there
> as the sky above the top floor of a tenement
> is nearer
> which is what the ancients meant by heaven
> to be with someone
> not just waiting wherever you are.[14]

O'Hara's "Personism" also extends to objects and becomes "animism." This is particularly true of parts of New York City: Fifth and Park avenues have a love-lorn conversation and Grand Central Station speaks:

> The wheels are inside me thundering.
> They do not churn me, they are inside. . . .
> Now I am going to lie down
> like an expanse of marble floor
> covered with commuters and information:
> it is my vocation, you believe that,
> don't you? . . .
> On rainy days I ache as if a train
> were about to arrive, I switch my tracks.[15]

Grand Central Station has not only become alive, it has become O'Hara himself.

Donald Allen's editing of O'Hara's *Collected Poems* is a considerable scholarly achievement, since O'Hara was careless with manuscripts; yet because of the book's size and the uneven quality of the poems, the reader might find a selection such as *Lunch Poems* a better introduction. And yet, in making a selection from O'Hara, different poems (because of their occasional nature) stand out on different readings. O'Hara in his praise for the Ordinary sometimes seems actually to aim for superficiality, just as the Abstract Expressionist painters aimed for "flatness." O'Hara wrote casually, often in a room full of people; the result was sometimes merely weak verse.

In addition to his achievement of urban romanticism, O'Hara left a "staggering load" to many younger poets: his apparently casual tone was liberating for some; others, however, began to pass off as poems slack chat about the trivia of their daily lives, or contrived bizarre word

stews without the internal tension that holds O'Hara's best poems
together.

If the New York poets are each as individual as New York taxi drivers,
then with Frank O'Hara at the wheel we cruise through Greenwich
Village with occasional side trips out to Fire Island. John Ashbery
drives us down deserted back streets between huge locked warehouses
with occasional glimpses of the harbor, then stops and soliloquizes
about his driving, his poor sense of direction and the tricks perspective
can play and asks us if we really want to go to the destination we had
requested.

> So going around cities
> To get to other places you found
> It all on paper but the land
> Was made of paper processed
> To look like ferns, mud or other
> Whose sea unrolled its magic
> Distances and then rolled them up
> Its secret was only a pocket. . . .
>   . . . and the map
> Carefully peeled away and not torn
> Was the light, a tender but tough bark
> On everything.[16]

O'Hara is casual, open, revealing; he once said of the technical apparatus of his poems, "That's just common sense: if you're going to buy
a pair of pants you want them to be tight enough so everyone will
want to go to bed with you."[17] Ashbery can be formal, hermetic,
secretive: he often slides a deliberate barrier between himself and his
readers like the glass shield protecting a New York taxi driver from his
passengers.

In Ashbery's poems there are constant echoes of other, secret dimensions, like chambers resounding behind hollow panels of an old
mansion rumored to contain secret passages (which our guide emphatically denies exist). Ashbery both hunts for these secrets and tries to
conceal them. "The Skaters," for example, opens with a description of

ice skaters that is matter-of-fact until "the water surface ripples, the whole light changes," and skaters and readers alike are plunged through the surface into the unknown.[18] "One average day / you may never know / How much is pushed back into the night, nor what / may return. . . ."[19] A heretic among contemporary poets who glory in "confessional" poetry, Ashbery even questions the value of "openness."[20]

Often these secrets are conveyed in code, secret messages hidden in the everyday. Code is a metaphor for the special language of poetry, into which Ashbery ciphers his secrets. He outlines two of his main methods of coding: "I thought if I could put it all down, that would be one way. And next the thought came to me that to leave it all out would be another, and truer, way."[21] "Leaving out" is a method which he frequently uses in earlier poems, where the connections among diverse apparent topics of his poems seem to have been erased. "I am not ready / To line phrases with the costly stuff of explanation. . . . / Except to say that the carnivorous / Way of these lines is to devour their own nature, leaving / Nothing but a bitter impression of absence. . . ."[22] He compares his literary method of "leaving out" to the natural process of forgetfulness which has its own concealed logic.[23]

Ashbery's other method of coding, "putting it all down," also has a parallel in a natural process of the mind: dreams, which often seem like cluttering an attic with everything imaginable. This use of "dream-work" gives Ashbery, like other New York poets, an affinity with the Surrealists. Ashbery's abrupt shifts from topic to topic derail the reader's logical expectations. Dreams use the same method to short-circuit the censorship of the waking mind. Ashbery has said: "[In poetry] I would also like to reproduce the power dreams have of persuading you that a certain event has a meaning not logically connected with it, or that there is a hidden relationship among disparate objects."[24] Dreams, then, are *active* and, despite their apparently ragbag inclusion of bits and pieces, reveal a secret code, a "hidden relationship among disparate objects." In this way dreams are like poems, particularly many of Ashbery's poems, which require the reader to relax and let the images flow over him or her, and yet at the same time to stay alert for hidden connections and look for the secret code. In another heresy (for his time), Ashbery even says that dreams, and perhaps poems, with their satisfactions of desire, may be preferable to transitory sex.[25]

How can Ashbery reveal to a reader this secret code which is in his poetry without feeling vulnerable?

> . . . . there is in that gaze a combination
> Of tenderness, amusement and regret, so powerful
> In its restraint that one cannot look for long.
> The secret is too plain. The pity of it smarts,
> Makes hot tears spurt: that the soul is not a soul,
> Has no secret, is small, and it fits
> Its hollow perfectly: its room, our moment of attention.[26]

Again, here is a typical New York poem focusing on the present, on "our moment of attention." Ashbery's later work has often had the tone of a letter—a form which seems to have released him from certain inhibitions. "This should be a letter / Throwing you a minute to one side, / Of how this tossing looks harmonious from a distance, / Like sea or the tops of trees, and how / Only when one gets closer is its sadness small and appreciable. / It can be held in the hand."[27] This one-to-one (and ephemeral) form allows Ashbery to reveal himself without making his private life a public spectacle. While introspective and autobiographical, Ashbery is not "confessional" in the way that Lowell, Plath and Ginsberg are.

What secrets does Ashbery reveal in poems that use devices similar to forgetfulness, dreams and letters? Until recently, the secrets we might have expected at the culmination of most ambitous poems on philosophical questions would have been some revelation of the divine. But, as Auden pointed out in his foreword to *Some Trees*, Ashbery is a poet in a secular age. Now, when atheism is orthodox, theology has become as abstract and figureless as an Abstract Expressionist painting. Although Ashbery calls to the "old heavens," he does not expect an answer: "For I am condemned to drum my fingers / On the closed lid of this piano, this tedious planet, earth, / As it winks to you through the aspiring, growing distances, / A last spark before the night."[28] Ashbery's secrets, so painfully and tortuously unveiled, are not one single, concrete truth and will vary from reader to reader; indeed he often contradicts himself, even within the same poem.

One secret Ashbery discloses is the very fact that secrets exist: not only is our age scientific and secular, but much of our poetry, particularly that influenced by Williams and by the New York poets, is emphatically grounded in the commonplace, the ordinary. Ashbery's concern with the mysterious and the transcendental, in addition to the everyday, contrasts with the poems of his friend, Frank O'Hara. When the sun, representing the source of O'Hara's poetic inspiration, speaks to him, it uses the jocular voice of another guy trying to wake him up. In Ashbery's poems, the fluid changes of subject signal to us that the hermetic glass bubble within which we try to contain "the real world" artificially is fragile and distorted: ". . . there is error in so much precision."[29] Soon "The balloon pops, the attention / Turns dully away."[30] By pushing us beyond our assumptions about reality, Ashbery moves decisively out of bounds.

At the same time as he affirms the sharply focused convex mirror which represents the ordering force of art and its opening of mystical dimensions, Ashbery turns away from its demands which impede life and he questions the restrictions art imposes on life, which is untidy. Sometimes Ashbery has attempted to reproduce the randomness of life through surreal automatic writing in books such as *Vermont Notebooks* and *The Tennis Court Oath*. However appealing automatic writing may be in theory, the result is not poetry: *Vermont Notebooks* is a relentlessly banal collection of lists and trivia, and most readers will punctuate *The Tennis Court Oath* with oaths more commonly heard on tennis courts when one's partner persists in serving outside the line.

In addition to revealing that secrets exist, Ashbery questions the process of our perception through poetry and reveals the secret of that perception by showing himself at work on the poem. This is both the subject and central metaphor of his long poem "Self-Portrait in a Convex Mirror," which is partly a description of the strange painting in which Parmigianino copied his reflection onto a wooden hemisphere the same size as his convex mirror. When the reader is allowed backstage, into the cluttered studio, and the poet reveals himself at work, there is always a risk of breaking the spell. (This is a flaw in many of Berryman's Dream Songs.) Ashbery avoids this by constantly turning his curious mirror to shift its focus and keep us hypnotized. "We have surprised him / At work, but no, he has surprised us / As he works."[31] One surprise, one secret, is that within the expanded present of this poem we and Ashbery and Parmigianino are all staring into a peculiar mirror that, like art, both focuses and distorts reality.

This simple reality, the ordinary world before it was distorted, Ashbery nominates as another of his secrets. "This nondescript, never-to-be defined daytime is / The secret of where it takes place. . . . / Today has that special, lapidary / Todayness that the sunlight reproduces / Faithfully in casting twig-shadows on blithe / Sidewalks. No previous day would have been like this." [32]

Certainly an important secret which Ashbery is very anxious to conceal, yet which constantly obsesses him, is his own self-portrait and what it reveals about him. The world for Ashbery is a hall of mirrors whose polished surfaces continually reflect, magnify and fragment his own image. These mirrors attract him, yet he feels compelled to shatter even their pleasantest illusions, such as the island in "The Skaters" ("bananas and spoonbread in the shadows of the old walls"), which he dispels with: "In reality of course the middle-class apartment I live in is nothing like a desert island. / Cozy and warm it is, with a good library and record collection. / Yet I feel cut off from life in the streets." His awareness of illusion enables him to endure it, to face the potentially grotesque and terrifying images of himself in the distorting mirrors, and even to look again: "Another time I thought I could see myself. / This too proved illusion, but I could deal with the way / I kept returning on myself like a plank / Like a small boat blown away from the wind." [33]

Perhaps the ultimate secret for Ashbery is poetry itself: a code as mysterious in its source as the snowflakes which represent it: "This, thus, is a portion of the subject of this poem / Which is in the form of falling snow. . . ." [34] What is significant is not each single flake or the entire storm but the rhythm of the shifting focus between the two. This shift is invisible and elusive, like the secret code that crystallizes into Ashbery's poetry.

Having decoded some general outline of these secrets within Ashbery's thicket of contradictions, the reader is entitled to ask: "How much work should I reasonably be expected to do before enjoying a poem? How obscure can a poet be when 'illustrating opacity' [35] without confounding his readers?" The danger of boredom and exasperation is a real one, particularly when Ashbery's style, while pleasant enough, is not outstandingly musical and relies on imagery for its effects. Sometimes his exposition of abstract philosophical issues is rather bloodless. Yet in his mature work his quicksilver images fascinate us, and his lines pace forward with inevitability and authority. By exploring intellectual questions deeply and attempting to discover an artistic order, Ashbery has taken a stand against the neo-Dadaists of the sixties; he is a very traditional poet who has affinities with Stevens and Rilke. Yet by moving beyond the bounds imposed by traditional ideas of form and opening his poetry to the voices of forgetfulness, dreams, letters and secret codes, Ashbery is at the same time one of our most experimental and unrestricted poets. He is like a Renaissance alchemist who can perform the boldest experiments because he claims the authority of the most ancient texts. In fact, Ashbery has described a chemical experiment which produces a fountain of flame that effervesces balls of fire and then related it to his writing technique:

In my day we used to make "fire designs," using a saturated
    solution of nitrate of potash.
Then we used to take a smooth stick, and using the solution as ink,
    draw with it on sheets of white tissue paper.
Once it was thoroughly dry, the writing would be invisible.
By means of a spark from a smoldering match ignite the potas-
    sium nitrate at any part of the drawing.
First laying the paper on a plate or tray in a darkened room.
The fire will smolder along the line of the invisible drawing
    until the design is complete.[36]

Kenneth Koch is at first glance just as much a surrealist as the other New York poets. But soon it is apparent that he is cleverly piling up his images not into the serious *croquembouche* of the French Surrealists but into good old American custard-pie slapstick. Koch's irreverent wit distinguishes him from O'Hara and Ashbery, who are usually grouped with Koch as the "Big Three" of the New York poets. Rather like Woody Allen, Koch can be quite zany in a particularly New York deadpan style. In a long poem about misunderstandings, he says: "I thought Axel's Castle / was a garage; / And I had beautiful dreams about it, too—sensual, mysterious / mechanisms: horns honking, wheels turning. . . ."[37]

    The Ordinary, which other New York poets so revere, Koch tips

upside down and shakes silly. Williams himself doesn't escape as Koch
parodies "This Is Just to Say":

> I gave away the money that you had been saving to live on for the
>   next ten years.
> The man who asked for it was shabby
> and the firm March wind on the porch was so juicy and cold. [38]

Koch has written books about teaching poetry to children and to old
people and teaches at Columbia University. His satires are more than
mere jokes: they have a serious purpose of literary and social criticism.
He is especially adroit at pushing the trendy concerns of our Present
Moment to their absurd extremes, as in "The Artist," his parodies of
South American poets and his poem about poets' feuds, "Fresh Air":
"Summer in the trees! 'It is time to strangle several bad poets. . . .' /
Here on the railroad train, one more time, is the Strangler. / He is
going to get that one there, who is on his way to a poetry reading. /
Agh! Biff! A body falls to the moving floor. . . . / Here is the
Strangler dressed in a cowboy suit / Leaping from his horse to an-
nihilate the students of myth!" [39]

Koch has attempted long poems and a comic epic, *Ko, Or a
Season on Earth*, which is not entirely successful, since its effects tend
to dissipate as it lengthens. More rewarding are the shorter poems in
his collections *Thank You and Other Poems* and *The Pleasures of
Peace*. His earlier poems show a certain amount of influence from
Kenneth Patchen (and, to a lesser extent, Marianne Moore). Although
some of Koch's poems do not move beyond light verse, he has a glint-
ing eye for the details of human folly and an exuberant imagination
that make him refreshing reading.

The term "New York poets," meaning confined to New York City, is
least apt when applied to James Schuyler. His poems often dwell on
minute details of nature such as the vein in a sumach leaf: ". . .
among the tumbled rocks—a / man-made scree below a house— / a
dull green sumach blade / slashed with red clearer than / blood a
skyblue red a first / fingertap, a gathering, a climax." [40] Winter, and
the pivot of the seasons, is a theme he returns to again and again.
Schuyler's natural world is not merely a conventional lush summer

pastoral, but in its ice and encompassing snow has something of the concrete city about it. He is adept at merging the country and the city, as in:

> beautiful New
> York sky harder
> so much than
> soft walls you see here around
> it shadowy lamp
> lighted plaster
> smoothed by a hand
> wielded trowel and
> roller painted
> by hand: Puerto
> Rican blue pressed
> tin ceiling sky
> up into and on
> which a white cup
> (more of a mug)
> falls, falls up—
> ward and crack
> splits into
> two glazed
> clay clouds [41]

This easy joining of nature and artifice distinguishes Schuyler from O'Hara, for whom they were irreconcilable opposites. Schuyler has for years been a friend and collaborator with the other New York poets, and he shares their use of surrealism. Although not as bizarre as some others, his poems still have many strange moments, and these surreal elements give his metaphors freshness: "An orange devours / the crusts of clouds and you, / getting up, put on / your daily life / grown somewhat shabby, worn / but comfortable, like old jeans: at the least, / familiar. . . ." [42]

Schuyler's relaxed skill which widens these metaphors is based on "a sudden wonderful feeling of accepting things as they are, even the things you don't like." [43] Even in one of his rare political poems, "Scarlet Tanagers," the pro-war veterans on the march are portrayed without rancor or cliché. The immediate moment, and everything in

it, is charged with significance for James Schuyler, as it is for Frank
O'Hara and John Ashbery. "All things are real / no one a symbol." [44]
This immediacy gives an intensity, yet classic simplicity, to some of
Schuyler's finest work to date—the sequence "Loving You" at the
close of *The Crystal Lithium.*

> The leaves—
> it's almost
> fall—look
> to last for
> ever—they will
> come tumbling
> down. I'm glad
> we are not
> leaves, or even
> trees whose twigs
> mesh. We are—
> you are you,
> I am I, and
> we mesh. And
> to ourselves
> we speak our
> thoughts and
> touch and that
> is love, isn't
> it? [45]

James Schuyler's poems have a presence, clarity and emotional
openness which are a culmination of the best in the New York movement.

The original New York poets influenced a second generation who appeared in the sixties. The best of these younger poets did not merely
reproduce the New York style but used it to launch themselves on
similar but divergent courses, and it has become increasingly difficult
to categorize poets as purely "New York." The legacy of the original
New York poets has been mixed but undeniably strong. Their surrealism has meant freedom to use words and images without the logical

restrictions of the conscious mind. The relaxed style of the younger New York poets, similar to ordinary talk, is suited to readings where a poem must be grasped by the audience on first hearing. A number of cafes, such as Le Metro, started to hold regular readings, and the church of St. Mark's-in-the-Bouwerie began a well-publicized Poetry Project in the late sixties. Unfortunately, for certain poets the automatic writing of the Surrealists became automatic talking at poetry readings, and their poems were simply self-indulgent. This fashion for automatic writing raises the question of what a poet should publish. Should every draft, notebook and experiment be presented in book form as finished work so that the poet can have a wide response to whatever new direction he or she may take? This argument has some appeal, and no one would want to set limits to the possibilities a poet can explore. Yet formal publication of experiments implies that they are meant to be permanent. They can be misunderstood not only by readers (who may be discouraged by the necessary obscurities and imperfections) but also by simple-minded followers, who happily repeat their master's cast-off styles like puppies dragging old shoes out of closets. How marvelous if every poet had a publisher waiting to print anything he or she wrote! Yet this can never be the case, and a poet who adopts an aesthetic of experiment must exercise judgment and ask: "Do I really want people to read these poems ten or a hundred years from now? Are they really worth cutting down a tree to get the paper to print them on?"

A related problem of the New York legacy to younger poets is the emphasis on the ordinary and the present. Weaker poets had no inhibitions against presenting as poems ramblings which were as banal as lethargic conversations on crossed telephone lines and which, in the form of "list poems," sunk to the nadir of boredom. On the other hand, this focus on present time and ordinary things encouraged poets to find subjects for poems in their daily lives.

New York poetry arouses responses of love or hate as extreme as the city itself. But no one who wants to understand the younger poets writing now can afford to ignore the influence of New York poetry— for it is one of the dominant sources of style and experiment in America today.

7

The American Blue Toad Swallows a Spanish Fly

The most savage and specific attack on the literary pretensions and prejudices of the fifties came from Robert Bly's magazine *The Sixties*. When this magazine first appeared in 1958, it was called *The Fifties*; then its name changed to *The Sixties*, then to *The Seventies*. I shall refer to it generally as *The Sixties*, because this was the decade in which most of its issues appeared and whose topics it discussed. *The Sixties* printed skilled parodies (sometimes even of its own favorites), the section "Madame Tussaud's Wax Museum" for "archaic and decrepit" poetry written by contemporary poets and an "Award of the Blue Toad" to any literary bigwig considered to be overweeningly pompous:

> THE ORDER OF THE BLUE TOAD is herewith awarded to Norman Cousins, editor of the *Saturday Review*, for putting out a boring, stupid magazine. . . . The *Saturday Review* now has "Quarterly Round-ups" of poetry. There is something very funny about this. It is beginning to resemble a medical journal devoting its efforts to reviewing basketball games. Norman Cousins' efforts to prevent people from bending to the Atomic Energy Commission seem absurd when the magazine itself bends to every wind—it is eager to shift its

whole format at the first breath from long-playing records, achievements in children's books, travel, stereophonics; what next? Therefore, we say that if Cousins wants to bore people to death and still get rich, he will have to accept insults. We therefore award him The Blue Toad, painted on a background of bedroom slippers, couched and rampant. The Toad is riding a fast turntable, and croaking scientific maxims.[1]

Some establishment magazines, such as *The New Republic*, were so incensed by *The Sixties'* outrageous attacks on the famous that they refused to accept ads for it. But *The Sixties* published more than just ax-murders of the academy: its parodies required close examination of the victims' conventions, it accepted the use of literary criticism (although not the loathed New Criticism) and it featured extensive analyses of the work of younger poets, as well as their poems and numerous translations from foreign poets.

Certain poets published much of their early work in *The Sixties* and share enough of its ideas to be considered together in this chapter: among them were Robert Bly, James Wright and James Dickey. Other poets had a similar outlook, although they may not always have appeared in *The Sixties* or been approved by Robert Bly. The major preoccupation of these poets is a journey to the interior: both to the interior of their native America and to the primitive interiors of their own minds. Within these interiors, which had been out of bounds for the restrained poets of the fifties, the *Sixties* poets have hoped to find their "New Worlds," so we shall refer to them as "American Interior" poets.

As we have seen, a new group of poets feels more able to attack the establishment when armed with the authority of a third group which is often older and / or foreign, but which is no longer threatening to the younger poets. Like Hercules, protected by wearing the invulnerable skin of the lion of Nemea which he had strangled, young poets when armored in older theories can then sally forth to slay other monsters. The American Interior poets found their Nemean lion skin in the work of South American and Spanish poets such as Neruda and Lorca. Hispanic-American literature provided a precedent for *The Sixties'* attack on mannered and formal verse. From about 1888 to 1916, a movement called *modernismo* "modernism" was dominant in Latin America. Intellectually and technically refined, it opposed the effusions of "bourgeois romanticism" with an aristocratic ideal of art for art's sake and a *fin-de-siècle* love of the exotic. *Modernismo* poets thus had some resemblance to the French Symbolists, to Eliot and early Pound, and to the American academics of the fifties. Later, Hispanic-American poets such as Neruda, Lorca, Velarde and Vallejo wanted a poetry based on the urgent realities of their world. Neruda called for "an impure poetry," "worn with the hand's obligations, as by acids, steeped in sweat and in smoke, smelling of lilies and urine, spattered diversely by the trades that we live by, inside the law or beyond it."[2] In a poem translated in *The Sixties* Enrique González Martínez demanded (albeit in a sonnet) an end to elegant verse: "Take this swan with puffy plumage, and wring his neck." Martínez preferred the intelligent owl who "does not have the elegance of the swan, but his troubled / Eye, which pierces into the darkness, reads / The mysterious book of the silence of night."[3]

These same Hispanic-American poets also advocated a return to the interior of America, *mundonovismo* ("new worldism"). The fiery, rich, fragrant realities of Latin America were too powerful for these poets to ignore, and they became a "South American dream" in such poems as Neruda's *Canto General* which, while visionary, did not ignore that earthly Eden's serpents, such as the United Fruit Company. The techniques of these new Hispanic-American poets were not neatly turned phrases and rhetoric, but startling surreal images, sudden as a tropical thunderstorm.

For many intellectuals in the United States during the late fifties and early sixties, Latin America was an emotional El Dorado, as Italy was for the Romantics in nineteenth-century Germany. Politically, the exploits of Che Guevera were followed avidly, and he was apotheosized in badges and tee shirts. Cuba was extolled as a New World where social injustice would be eradicated. *El Corno Emplumado* (a bilingual magazine published between 1961 and 1969 which formed an important link between new writers in the U.S. and in Latin America) said in an editorial: "Our children will not see the world we know. The change is upon us, in our hands and in our mountains and in our cities—brute and sure. . . . In Cuba, the real mirror in which we care to see ourselves reflected. . . ."[4] There was a growing cultural consciousness of and on the part of the large numbers of U.S. citizens of Hispanic ancestry. So it was no accident that the covers of *The Sixties* showed a mounted conquistador. The American Interior poets' version of "new worldism" was a return to essential America.

Not only were their settings unmistakably American (the Midwest of Bly, Wright, Niedecker and Stafford; the South of Dickey), but their outlook was also rural and had precedents in the Populist movement. There were urban versions of this proletarian viewpoint in the work of Galway Kinnell and Louis Simpson.

This widespread interest in undeveloped South America and in the interior of the United States paralleled the contemporary fascination with another "New World"—the interior of the mind, the non-rational worlds of dreams and myths. Bly commends Neruda's poems because "His imagination sees the hidden connections between conscious and unconscious substances with such assurance that he hardly bothers with metaphors—he links them by tying their hidden tails. He is a new kind of creature moving about under the surface of everything."[5] Once again Surrealism left its mark on contemporary American poetry. But this Surrealism was transmitted to the American Interior poets via Hispanic-American poets and differed from the French Surrealism which had affected the New York poets. For the American Interior poets' surrealism had not been derived from art critical theory (indeed *The Sixties* was almost completely unillustrated) and they were also more concerned with people and politics than were the French Surrealists or the New York poets.

As his magazine was typical of its decade, so Robert Bly's poetry voices the sixties' concerns: both interior and exterior, personal and social. Although mysticism and politics may appear to be incompatible, Bly maintains that political awareness is an escapable result of intensified personal consciousness. ". . . The poet's main job is to penetrate that husk around the American psyche, and since that psyche is inside *him* too, the writing of political poetry is like the writing of personal poetry, a sudden drive by the poet inward."[6] Bly not only attacked what he saw as tyrannical literary politics but was a relentless critic of nuclear testing and the Vietnam war. The demands for changes in U.S. society which Bly and many other people made in the sixties also had roots in the ideas of the Populist movement, which had its heyday in the Midwest in the 1890's and 1930's.

The other "outer world" which is the subject of so many of Bly's poems is the realm of nature. Looking at a tumbleweed brought in from the snow, he exclaims: "Brown and everywhere! It has leaped up on my desk like surf, or like a bull onto a cow! . . . And my sleeping senses are shouted at, called in from the back of my head, to look at it! . . . Taken from the deserted shore, it talks of queens sent away to live in cramped farmhouses, living in the dirt, and it talks of coffins and amazing arrows, no it is a love, some love we forget every day, it is my mother."[7] Bly earns his living as a farmer and translator, not as an academic, publisher or critic. The realities and loneliness of farm life, especially through the long Minnesota winter, haunt many of Bly's poems. A down-to-earth tone often appears in his writing and tempers his idealism with horse sense.

Yet all this practicality and activism notwithstanding, Bly's major commitment is to an inner reality, to exploring the self which lies beyond the bounds its own consciousness has built. Solitude, particularly that imposed by farm life, is fruitful for him. Night and sleep are not closures but openings into other worlds, into a self that is hidden, like "Water Under the Earth":

O yes, I love you, book of my confessions,
when the swallowed begins to rise from the earth again,
and the deep hungers from the wells.
So much is still inside me, like cows eating in a collapsed
    strawpile

all winter to get out.
Everything we need now is buried,
it's far back into the mountain,
it's under the water guarded by women.
These lines themselves are sunk to the waist in the dusk
    under the odorous cedars,
each rain will only drive them deeper,
they will leave a faint glow in the dead leaves.
You too are weeping in the low shade of the pine branches,
you feel yourself about to be buried too,
you are a ghost stag shaking his antlers in the herony light—
what is beneath us will be triumphant
in the cool air made fragrant by owl feathers.

I am only half-risen,
I see how carefully I have covered my tracks as I wrote,
how well I brushed over the past with my tail[8].

While Bly's voyages into the worlds of sleep and the unconscious link him with the Surrealists, his poems are not as bizarre as those of some other contemporary poets influenced by the Surrealists. Bly's fascination with dreams and areas of consciousness which had been out of bounds crystallizes in his use of myths. Unlike the academic poets, who employed myths for theme material or as metaphors, Bly considers myths to be embodiments of profound truths, and wants a poetry that performs a similar function. "I see in my own poetry and the poems of so many other poets alive now fundamental attempts to right our own spiritual balance, by encouraging those parts in us that are linked with music, with solitude, water, and trees, the parts that grow when we are far from the centers of ambition.[9]

Bly's tireless efforts to renew American poetry and to open it to Hispanic Surrealism have met with considerable success. His own poetry, although it occasionally suffers from the self-conscious application of concepts which became conventions among the American Interior poets, still retains its individual flavor and integrity.

The ideal of the American poet current during the sixties was that of the bard, who would represent his nation in the tradition of Walt Whitman. Yet James Dickey, whose outlook is probably typical of the majority of Americans, was, for that very reason, scorned by Whitman's many disciples. (The reputation of Robert Frost also plummeted among the intelligentsia because he was considered too "popular.") Dickey's *persona* is not that of a *poète maudit* at war with bourgois society but that of a regular guy from an ordinary background with problems and pleasures that could happen to anyone. His poems are not preoccupied with the difficulties of being a poet; indeed, he seems to regard poetry as an almost physical skill to be mastered, like archery. He aims for "a purely tribal poetry, something naive and utterly convincing, immediately accessible, animistic, communal, dancelike, entered into, participated in."[10] Dickey's poems touch the average person: both through subject matter and the ease of a literal understanding. In "The Bee" he describes his emotions, memories and, most characteristically, his actions when he has to catch his small son who has been stung by a bee and is running onto a busy highway:

> Old wingback, come
> To life. If your knee action is high

> Enough, the fat may fall in time   God damn
> You, Dickey, *dig*   this is your last time to cut
> And run   but you must give it everything you have
> Left, for screaming near your child is the sheer
> Murder of California traffic. . . .[11]

These gasping, broken lines echo the suspense and awful slow-motion feeling of an imminent accident. As in so many of Dickey's poems, the drama and urgency of his narrative sweep us along and carry us into a vivid world within the poem. Their narrative surface should not deceive the reader into thinking that Dickey's poems are obvious—they require a real emotional work-out. Often Dickey will confront the reader with dilemmas as painful as they are universal: a chronic disease, elderly parents, school friends lost or their lives squandered, the need to kill in war.

Unlike the mental dramas that gripped the Extremist poets, Dickey's struggles are not only emotional conflicts but actual physical battles for survival. In his wry "The Cancer Match," cancer and whiskey wrestle for control of his body. "Diabetes" reveals sugar as "Gangrene in white / Was in my wife's hand at breakfast / Heaped like a mountain. . . ."[12] In addition to these poems about personal survival against disease and war, there are many others where he deliberately pits himself against natural forces. His family's survival is also a preoccupation of Dickey's. In his own generation, his older brother died quite young of typhoid. To amuse his young son (now the same age as his dead brother), Dickey weaves on his fingers the string figures which his brother had made: "Mark how the brother must live, / who comes through the words of my mother."[13] Death also highlights the family strings, which it severs as Dickey leaves the tall glass hospital where his father lies dying. In the middle of the street Dickey stops and waves up to his father's window among the hundreds reflecting the sun: "I know that my father is there, / In the shape of his death still living. . . . / Lifts his arm out of stillness at last, / The light from the window strikes me, / And I turn blue as a soul, / As the moment when I was born. . . ."[14] Dickey also asks what his sons will inherit from him. At the same time, as he watches his son snorkel, he reminds himself: "And I must let you go, out of your gentle / Childhood into your own man suspended / In its body, slowly waving its feet / Deeper and deeper, while the dark grows. . . ."[15]

Survival of his nation is important to Dickey. His war poems do not glamorize war nor shrink from its horrific details, which are difficult for anyone who was not actually there to imagine. Sent to the Pacific in World War II while he was still a teenager, Dickey flew eighty-seven missions and was awarded the Silver Star and two Distinguished Flying Crosses. Yet in poems such as "The Firebombing" he sees the nightmare of war invade ordinary lives:

> All leashes of dogs
> Break under the first bomb, around those
> In bed, or late in the public baths: around those
> Who inch forward on their hands
> Into medicinal waters.
> Their heads come up with a roar
> Of Chicago fire. . . .[16]

With this poem and others in *Buckdancer's Choice* (1965) Dickey became highly controversial: he won the National Book Award but infuriated old friends like Robert Bly, who had previously published many of Dickey's poems and critical essays. "Suddenly at the age of forty-three we have a huge blubbery poet pulling out Southern language in long strings, like taffy, a toady to the government, supporting all movement toward Empire, a sort of Georgia cracker Kipling," fumed Bly, and castigated Dickey for lack of guilt and excessive detachment.[17] An earlier issue of *The Sixties*, Number 7, had praised Dickey's war-pilot poems. Bly refused to accept what he called "the New Critical brainwashing" that the pilot in "The Firebombing" is a *persona* but insisted that that figure must be judged as Dickey himself. Is "The Firebombing" detached and amoral? "It is this detachment, / This honored aesthetic evil, / The greatest sense of power in one's life, / That must be shed in bars, or by whatever / Means, by starvation / Visions in well-stocked pantries. . . ."[18] Guilt and identification are the real issues Bly and Dickey are disputing. Guilt was a cardinal virtue of the sixties, just as virginity was revered in the Middle Ages. Anyone born into white middle-class America was expected to feel guilty for collective crimes against blacks, Vietnamese, American Indians, women, and gays. Independent of the very real rights and wrongs of these issues, guilt became a social obligation among intellectuals. The sixties was an era of soulful Che Guevara posters in suburban bedrooms and bulging shopping bags printed with the Viet Cong flag. In Bly's poem about Vietnam, "The Teeth-Mother Naked at Last," he appears to identify more with the Vietnamese villagers than Dickey does with the Japanese in "The Firebombing." Yet Bly remains at a distance: through his extensive use of similes and metaphors (including one he attacks other poets for using to romanticize war, "red pins *blossoming* ahead of us")[19] and through the moral safety of his rhetoric—Bly and his audience are always conscientious Americans at a reading against the war, they are never really the bombers or the bombed.

Dickey's poem is more complex and more vivid. Although some reference to Vietnam may be inevitable, its bombing raid occurs during World War II, in the Pacific conflict which began with the Japanese surprise bombing of Pearl Harbor. Survival, as so often with Dickey, is the overt motive. Yet, that civilians have to be bombed with excruciating napalm, supposedly in self-preservation, is appalling—not only to the reader, but to the pilot, who twenty years later keeps experiencing flashbacks of his raid that now invade his own suburban comfort:

> I still have charge—secret charge—
> Of the fire developed to cling
> To everything: to golf carts and fingernail
> Scissors as yet unborn   tennis shoes
> Grocery baskets   toy fire engines
> New Buicks stalled by the half-moon
> Shining at midnight on crossroads   green paint
> Of jolly garden tools   red Christmas ribbons. . . .[20]

Nor can the pilot exorcise his guilt completely, for he admits that it is impossible for him (or anyone else) to be totally aware of another's suffering: "All families lie together, though some are burned alive. / The others try to feel / for them. . . ."[21] Bly condemns *Buckdancer's Choice*—"the subject of these poems is power, and the tone of the book is gloating—a gloating about power over others—and considers "Slavery Quarters" one of the most repulsive poems ever written in American Literature."[22] Dickey's attitude toward his southern inheritance as expressed in his poems is by no means as unambivalent as Bly claims. Yet Dickey is certainly not "groggy with guilt" either. While at Vanderbilt University he came under the lingering influence of the Fugitives and the southern Agarians, who included John Crowe Ransom, Robert Penn Warren and Allen Tate. They were against industrialization wrecking the old southern culture and favored a distributist agarian economy (ideas similar to those of the Populist Movement). Power and survival are certainly Dickey's subjects, American preoccupations and legitimate subjects for poetry. Power is a reality—it may corrupt, but a wise use of it is necessary for survival and for high achievement. Indeed, power through language is one of most poets' goals. Nor do poets shrink from the baser sorts of power: the ruthlessness of some poets on university committees and literary magazines makes Mafia dons look like little old ladies.

After comparing Dickey's and Bly's poems about napalm bombing we are left with a very uncomfortable conclusion: although Bly's stand against the Vietnam war was morally correct in the view of many readers, including myself, his poem is not as good as Dickey's "The Firebombing." Because the pilot is so thoroughly American, American readers inevitably identify with him, and there is no simple moral escape hatch. Dickey's poem is far more disturbing than Bly's and ultimately intensifies more our revulsion against the napalming of civilians (despite Dickey's public support of the Vietnam war). These two poems raise a major question: should poetry (or any art) aim to improve life and show an ideal, or should it merely reflect reality? Are these two purposes incompatible? This moral question has been particularly perplexing for poets in recent years.

The natural world is a vivid presence in all of Dickey's poems. Even in those poems whose main subject is an emotional struggle, nature is never merely a metaphor. In contrast, the skunks in Lowell's "Skunk Hour" are well drawn but still illustrations of feelings rather than beasts with an independent existence. Dickey's relation to the natural world is complex: on the one hand, it is his source of strength; on the other, it is a murderous adversary. The three sections of "On the Coosawatte," which describe a canoe trip on that Georgia river illustrate three of the many aspects of Dickey's relation to nature. In the first part the river flows through pine woods whose needles float so thickly on the water that Dickey and his companion feel they are going deep into the trees themselves. "As I taste the fretted light fall / Through living needles to be here / Like a word I can feed on forever.

. . ."[23] Through the dark of these trees he draws energy and the essence of being itself. But "Below Ellijay" the river suffers a gruesome change as it runs past a poultry slaughterhouse. The waste feathers clog the water and paste themselves onto the rocks, which become grim parodies of dead chickens. Nature, the stream corrupted by man, hinders the canoe with slimy feathers and offal; and in the third section of the poem the river attacks, breaks the canoe and hurls out its passengers. They float away in their life preservers and collapse exhausted on the bank. Found asleep by "a strange woods boy," Lucas Gentry, Dickey finally accepts the river's violent and nuturing aspects:

> Where we almost died takes on the settled repose
> Of that other where we lay down and met
> Our profoundest sleep
> Rising from it to us, as the battered sides
> Of the canoe gave deeper and deeper shade,
> And Lucas Gentry,
>
> Who may have been the accepting spirit of the place
> Come to call us to higher ground,
> Bent to raise
> Us from the sleep of the yet-to-be-drowned,
> There, with the black dream of the dead canoe
> Over our faces.[24]

It is interesting to compare this and Dickey's other poems about the Georgia landscape with those of a predecessor, Sidney Lanier, a Georgia poet who lived from 1842 to 1881. In Lanier's much-anthologized "Song of the Chattahoochee," another Georgia stream runs through the hills: the rushes and shady trees try to persuade it to stay with them, but it hurries down to water the farms and turn the mills of man, who has not yet polluted it. Similarly, in Lanier's "Marshes of Glynn," "belief overmasters doubt" and his soul seems "suddenly free" as he sees "Ye marshes, how candid and simple and nothing-withholding and free / Ye publish yourselves to the sky and offer yourselves to the sea!"[25] Dickey in "The Salt Marsh" loses all sense of direction but discovers that "Green panic may finally give / Way to another sensation," as the wind bends down the obscuring grasses:

>And nothing prevents your bending
>With them, helping their wave
>Upon wave upon wave upon wave
>By not opposing,
>By willing your supple inclusion
>Among fields without promise of harvest,
>In their marvelous, spiritual walking
>Everywhere, anywhere.[26]

Both poets achieve a concord with nature, although for Dickey it is more of a struggle, because of his time and his temperament.

Nature for Dickey is not only a sustainer and destroyer but a gateway into other worlds and other beings. When these other beings appear, they are all the more striking because of their homely roots. In "Chenille" the animals his grandmother appliqués onto a quilt come to life: "Deer, rabbits and birds, / Red whales and unicorns, / Winged elephants, crowned ants: / Beasts that cannot be thought of / By the wholly sane. . . ."[27] These other beings, other worlds that glide beneath the surface of daylight reality are a common preoccupation of American Interior poets. Dickey's strong sense of natural realities not only makes his ventures out of bounds less incomprehensible than those of other surrealist poets, but makes his poems even more uncanny. In fact, he has stated his preference for "country surrealism."[28]

The major problem with James Dickey's poems is their length— sometimes their sprawl and repetition destroy the dramatic tension which is one of their great strengths. One critic, Norman Silverstein, has suggested that Dickey ought to stick to fiction. Certainly length does cause problems in some poems, but in his better work it is a characteristic which the reader can accept from having become accustomed to it, as to a friend whose stories are spun-out but spellbinding. In addition to their dramatic flair, James Dickey's poems also are honest: without self-consciousness or subterfuge, he shows how many people genuinely live and feel. With only occasional bombastic lapses, he dovetails into this authenticity a realm of forceful but unpretentious imagination. Younger poets would do well to reappraise their opinions of Dickey (which may have been formed on the basis of politics and life-style); for his down-to-earth yet fantastic poems are at the core of a long American tradition.

James Wright's poems focus on his country, his family and himself. America evoked both nostalgia and dread in him. During the sixties he wrote a number of outspoken political poems, such as "Eisenhower's Visit to Franco 1959," many of which appeared in Robert Bly's magazine. But he never renounced his country; visiting Europe he saw all the famous sights, such as the portal of Chartres cathedral, in terms of America: "this cracking blossom is my second America."[29] Much of the time America was summed up for him by hoboes and the poor, often in grim industrial cities. From his southern Ohio childhood he paraded riverside characters such as Jimmy Leonard. Poverty and helplessness in the face of huge corporations weighed down his friends and family. Wright remembered his father as a

> Strange bird,
> His song remains secret.
> He worked too hard to read books.
> He never heard how Sherwood Anderson
> Got out of it, and fled to Chicago, furious to free himself
> From his hatred of factories.
> My father toiled fifty years
> At Hazel-Atlas Glass,
> Caught among girders that smash the kneecaps
> Of dumb honyaks.
> Did he shudder with hatred in the cold shadow of grease?
> Maybe. But my brother and I do know
> He came home quiet as the evening.[30]

The constraints of poverty extended to the pinched human relationships that "starve and freeze." James Wright refused to be sucked into the emotional whirlpool of a family funeral:

> When we get back, the wagon will be gone,
> The porchlight empty in the wind, no doubt;
>   And everybody here,
> Who damned us for the conscience of a stone,
>   Will tell us to get out
> And do our sniffling in the dark somewhere. . . .

> Come here to me; I will not let you go
> To suffer on some relative's hard shoulder—
>   Weeping woman or man.
> God, I have died so many days ago,
>   The funeral began
> When I was born, and will go on forever. . . .[31]

Wright could also be nostalgic, even romantic, about his family and his birthplace: "White mares lashed to the sulky carriages / Trot softly / Around the dismantled fairgrounds / Near Buckeye Lake. / The sandstone blocks of a wellspring / Cool dark green moss. . . ."[32] There are quicksands of sentimentality in this kind of subject matter, and Wright sometimes jumped into them. His pictures of Ohio are fascinating, but occasionally unconvincing: for he shows us only the extremes—grotesques or pastorals, tramps or deer. He never attempted to construct poems on an epic scale out of his rural experience, as Olson did with his Gloucester poems or Edgar Lee Masters did with *Spoon River Anthology*. However, despite their flaws, Wright's Ohio poems are some of his best.

From these diverse images of his country and his family Wright was trying to construct a picture of himself. Often he identified not only with the poverty of his family, but also with the destitution and despair of hoboes: "I wonder how many old men last winter / Hungry and frightened by namelessness prowled / The Mississippi shore / Lashed blind by the wind, dreaming / Of suicide in the river."[33] Some of his poems, particularly those written in Minnesota, are reminiscent of Berryman. Wright's diffuse fears sometimes condensed into the dread that the precarious self he had constructed would be attacked by poverty, sickness, old age and death, as expressed in poems such as "In Terror of Hospital Bills." Interestingly, he coped with his fear of death by dreaming about his own burial: "So I waited, in my corridor. / I listened for the sea / To call me. / I knew that, somewhere outside, the horse / Stood saddled, browsing in the grass, / Waiting for me."[34] Because Wright's self-image was so largely dependent on exterior people and places, it was diffuse and fragile. Even when he lived in New York, part of him remained defensively provincial: "No, I ain't much. / The one tongue I can write in / Is my Ohioan."[35] This sense of being second-rate may have been one motive for his shift in style after 1971 to the looser, more surreal technique favored by the New

York poets. These later poems of Wright's are not always successful: frequently they are disjointed, the title is not congruent with the poem and they ramble ineffectually. Wright's poems before 1963 were marred by an excessive Romanticism and constricted by forms with heavy end rhymes. He counteracted these problems by using more colloquialisms and frank, even naturalistic details. Both Wright's early and late periods lack a sense of humor and the perspective that implies.

In some of the most moving poems of his middle period, Wright turned to nature as the solver of man's mistakes, as in the poem titled "Depressed by a Book of Bad Poetry, I Walk Toward an Unused Pasture and Invite the Insects to Join Me." This is very much in the American tradition of Thoreau and Whitman. And it is nature, finally, that stilled his horrors, even of death:

Once,
I was afraid of dying
In a field of dry weeds.
But now,
All day long I have been walking among damp fields,
Trying to keep still, listening
To insects that move patiently.
Perhaps they are sampling the fresh dew that gathers slowly
In empty snail shells
And in the secret shelters of sparrow feathers fallen on the earth.[36]

James Wright was an uneven poet, particularly in the last years before his early death in 1980. When he was bad, he could be mawkish and verbose, but there are many times when his great risks of sentimentality pay great dividends and he moves us by going straight to the heart of a human situation in lines that are simple but absolutely right.

Certain other poets' work might also be called American Interior, although they may not have been admired by Bly or printed in *The Sixties*. William Stafford's poems place him in spiritual company with the poets in this chapter, although he is something of a lone wolf. Born in Hutchinson, Kansas, he sets his poems in the Midwest, extols a country simplicity over city sophistication and shows traces of Populist philosophy. Sometimes he writes about social questions—not specifically political poems, but a quiet assertion of every person's equal rights: "Men should not claim, nor should they have to ask."[37] Stafford has an unerring ear for country speech in plain, unblinking poems, such as "On Quitting a Little College":

> By footworn boards, by steps
> that sagged years after the pride of workmen
> by things that had to *do* so long they now seemed right,
> by ways of acting so old they grooved the people
> (and all this among fields that never quit
> under a patient sky),
> I taught. And then I quit.[38]

His focus on his birthplace often centers on his family, and leads him to ponder his resemblance to them. In a poem about his mother he says: "My mother was afraid / and in my life her fear has hid. . . ."[39] Memories of his home town and landscape are the key that unlocks his inner world: "we are forced backwards into our dreams."[40] Sometimes this journey inward is a metamorphosis into an animal or a reflection of the deep self seen in the living, watching land. Stafford's surrealism, while not obviously irrational, is certainly spooky, particularly when he describes empty rooms and deserted houses, like "The Old Hammer Place":

> . . . no one in the world tonight is
> even thinking about that hollow house
> when the truck left years ago and the moaning
> seasons began to wander through the room, stirring
> vines and their shadows that grew in the dark.
>> I touch that wall, collapsing it there where
>> no one knows, by the quavering owl sound
>> in a forest no one knows. . . .
>> A *whole town might come shuddering back, that had*
>>> *disappeared*
>> *When a dark animal began to overcome the world*
>> *and a little bird came to sing our walls down.*[41]

Because he is haunted by these presences from other, interior worlds, Stafford is a wanderer, never entirely at home in the conventional waking world. He remembers "the canoe wilderness" with "hard fins prying out from the dark below."

> Often in society when the talk turns witty
> you think of that place, and can't polarize at all:
> it would be a kind of treason. The land fans in your head
> canyon by canyon, steep roads diverge.
> Representing far places you stand in the room,
> all that you know merely a weight in the weather.
>
> It is all right to be simply the way you have to be,
> among contradictory ridges in some crescendo of knowing. [42]

Stafford is both at home in the natural world, which is so much a part of himself, and a perpetual stranger, "Time's Exile," "who finds his way by sunflowers through the dark." [43]

Since *Traveling Through the Dark*, Stafford's second book, which won him the National Book Award in 1962, the intensity of his verse has diminished. This is partly a result of his simple style, which is not always inventive enough to follow the complexities of his ideas; these then appear in some poems as flat philosophical platitudes. Hopefully he will surmount this technical problem and again give us poems of freshness and strength.

A rural poet who has begun to have a certain underground following is Lorine Niedecker. Her similarity to the other poets in this chapter is one of outlook rather than style. Her poems are mostly very brief, consciously modeled on *haiku*, and she describes the poet's work as a "condensery." While her poems are not themselves surreal, her elliptical technique and identification with nature sometimes result in surreal juxtapositions. The lakes and marshes of Wisconsin, where she grew up and spent most of her life, provide her settings and subjects. Her father fished, her mother grew deaf and died while Lorine Niedecker was still young. They were poor and struggled hard, particularly in bad weather, as Niedecker imagines her mother describing:

> Well, spring overflows the land,
> floods floor, pump, wash machine
> of the woman moored to this low shore by deafness.
>
>> Good-bye to lilacs by the door
>> and all I planted for the eye.
>> If I could hear—too much talk in the world.
>> too much wind washing, washing
>> good black dirt away.
>
> Her hair is high.
> Big blind ears.
>
>> I've wasted my whole life in water.
>> My man's got nothing but leaky boats.
>> My daughter, writer, sits and floats.[44]

This marsh dominated Niedecker's consciousness, "the sloughs and sluices / of my mind / with the persons / on the edge."[45] There is also a streak of Populism in Niedecker's poems, such as her description of the rich girl's wedding: 'United for life to serve / silver. Possessed.'"[46] The reader's difficulty with Niedecker's poetry is its unreliable quality: verses with rhymes too gooey even for greeting cards are printed next to lyrics of a classical simplicity. Sometimes she is able to avoid the swamp of rhymes by imitating *haiku*; this, however, brings its own problems—a cramped archness and a lack of scope and energy. When Niedecker does succeed, it is often in poems about personal relationships (reminiscent of Emily Dickinson) which provide the tension missing in other poems. At her best, the homely details and realities of her life are economically and memorably captured:

>> Popcorn-can cover
>> screwed to the wall
>> over a hole
>>   so the cold
>> can't mouse in[47]

This rural, American Interior outlook which we have seen in the poets in this chapter is not confined to those who live in, and write about, the country. Louis Simpson, for instance, calls himself an "American peasant"; when in the Fifth Avenue apartment of a friend who is discussing politics, Simpson's mind wanders out the window to a dog who "must have discovered something / mixed with the odor of crankcase oil / and dust, a delirious / fragrance of sexual life."[48] Yet Simpson's feelings are more complex than a mere romantic longing for greenery: "In the city I pine for the country; / In the country I long for conversation—/ Our happy croaking."[49]

Simpson's dreams of the country are sometimes fantasies about "the old country"—the Russia his mother and relations emigrated from: ". . . . all my life I've been haunted / by Russia—a plain, / a cold wind from the *shtetl*."[50] He explores this inheritance, which is often painful, in terms of individuals. For these immigrants, and for Simpson himself, who was brought to the United States from Jamaica when he was fifteen, America was a Promised Land. How its reality does or does not match the American Dream preoccupies Simpson. He asks Walt Whitman's statue: "The Open Road goes to the used-car lot. / Where is the nation you promised? / . . . all the realtors, / Pickpockets, salesmen, and the actors performing / Official scenarios, / Turned a deaf ear, for they had contracted / American dreams. / . . . The future in ruins!"[51] Simpson is particularly caustic about the misery of well-off suburbanites, such as a friend his own age who has made a million dollars and lives in luxury. Yet "Bill and Marion" feel they are "missing out on life"; they separate and the household is broken up—even Bill's rare tropical fish is flushed down the toilet and his cherished Stevenson poster is burned in the fireplace "Because the moving men wanted to / and he didn't have the heart to refuse."[52] Affluent America's lack of heart, its failure of the will to say no to violence is attacked by Simpson in his political poems, which expose the moral sickness of sixties America. His conclusion is typical of his decade as he gazes at the Pacific: "How sad it is, the end of America! . . . . / Whitman was wrong about the People, / But right about himself. The land is within. / At the end of the open road we come to ourselves."[53]

Once again the journey to the interior of America becomes a journey to the interior of the self. Not only are words realities, and fantasies compelling, but dreams are the visible world. In "The Psyche of Riverside Drive" even the most sharply drawn menaces and fears of life in New York City dissolve in the powerful undercurrent of dream that pulls the poem out into the Caribbean, where "There is always some passionate race / that has just arrived in America / And a fragrance, *pimienta*, / the wind brings over the sea."[54] Technically, Simpson's poems have a narrative, and are not surreal in that they are not automatic writing; however, there is always a strong stream of fantasy that tows the reader to unexpected shores. Simpson's later poems have sometimes been rather prosy and suffered from a certain lack of music. However, these failings are more than outweighed by his wit, which jokes even at the expense of himself and his friends. His quotable, epigrammatical style is underlined by his almost photographic portraits of ordinary people and their lives.

How then does Simpson survive in the flawed American Dream? "One way to live is to tell stories."[55] Talking with a friend who works in a mental hospital, Simpson says:

> I too have my cases:
> hands, eyes, voices, ephemera.
> They want me to see how they live.
> They single me out in a crowd, at a distance,
> the one face that will listen
> to any incoherent, aimless story.
> Then for years they hang around—
> "Hey listen!"—tugging at a nerve.
> Like the spirits the Buddhists call
> "hungry ghosts." And when they sense an opening,
> rush in, So they are born
> and live. So they continue.
>
> There is something in disorder that calls to me.
> Out there beyond the harbor
> where, every night, the lighthouse
> probes the sea with its feathery beam,
> something is rising to the surface.
> It lies in the darkness breathing.[56]

This is Simpson's greatest asset: he does not merely reproduce disorder by surreal techniques, but he tries to tell each individual's story, to feed the hungry ghost at the boundaries of the American Dream.

Galway Kinnell is another poet whose journeys take him to the interior of America and of his own mind. Despite his much anthologized poem about the Lower East Side of New York, "The Avenue Bearing the Initial of Christ into the New World," he writes from an essentially rural viewpoint: even the polyglot metropolis of New York he reduces to its essentials as a small village: "Our little lane, what a kingdom it was!" [57] In "Freedom, New Hampshire," written in memory of his brother, Kinnell recalls their country childhood with affectionate but open eyes. His country poems are rustic but dignified. Kinnell is not surreal in his methods, but he does struggle to discover a reality beyond the waking one: "In the heart of a man / There sleeps a green worm / That has spun the heart about itself, / And that shall dream itself black wings / One day to break free into the beautiful black sky." [58]

While he shares some concerns, such as violence and Vietnam, with the other American Interior poets, Kinnell's major themes are the problems of mortality and grace. He has tenaciously wrestled with the "nightmare of mortality" for many years, culminating in his masterful *Book of Nightmares*, published in 1971. Modeled loosely on Rilke's *Duino Elegies*, Kinnell's book also stresses the primary importance of here-and-now reality, even while he attempts to go beyond its bounds. The first section begins with Kinnell trying to light a wet fire and continues with the birth of his daughter, Maud, and then with his attempts to comfort her when she awakens from a nightmare and to prepare her for later, waking nightmares: "And then / you shall open / this book, even if it is the book of nightmares." [59] This is Kinnell's best book to date, partly because of his changes of scale, such as from a child's nightmare to the international nightmare of Vietnam. He also startles us by sudden contrasts between horror and tenderness, as when the southern sheriff fingerprints civil rights demonstrators:

Of that time in a Southern jail,
when the sheriff, as he cursed me
and spat, took my hand in his hand, rocked
from the pulps the whorls
and tented archways into the tabooed realm, that underlife
where the canaries of the blood are singing, pressed
the flesh-flowers
into the dirty book of the
police blotter, afterwards what I remembered most
was the care, the almost loving,
animal gentleness of his hand on my hand. [60]

Kinnell tackles ambitious subjects with a wide scope, yet he always makes them real and related to real people. His early end rhymes changed to tense, pared-down lines whose force comes from their vivid imagery. At his best he shows the grotesque and human caught in huge issues, like an idiosyncratic gargoyle on an immense cathedral.

Have the American Interior poets of *The Sixties* anything to say to the eighties and nineties? Despite their occasional lapses into portentousness and their own conventions, the answer must be an emphatic yes: their explorations of the interiors of America and of themselves are not only the result of a turbulent decade but essential expressions of a deep and historical current in American literature. Their finest poems combine the immense richness both of the exterior reality of America and of the interiors of their own imaginations.

8

"The Voyage of Recovery":
Recent British Poetry

"There are no American poets in this anthology. . . . Contemporary American poetry . . . thanks to the excessive interest taken in it by American universities, is now an industry rather than an art. . . ."[1]

"With few exceptions (mainly Ted Hughes) nothing much new seems to have happened in English poetry since Lawrence laid down his pen and died."[2]

These are only two salvos in the War for Independence which the Americans and British are still fighting on the poetry front. Recently the Americans have proclaimed victory, and even some Britons have conceded defeat. This American prominence is the reverse of, and a reaction to, years of British cultural colonialism. Even after two hundred years of political independence the common language is still called English. Americans now dominate poetry in English after the innovations of Eliot and Pound (linguistically American, although expatriates)—through the multitude of American universities which have provided secure livelihoods for the academic poets and New Critics of the fifties, and through the initiatives of movements such as the Black Mountain, Beat, Extremist, New York and American Interior. Although the Poetic War for Independence has been largely won, there is still a great deal of American anxiety about British poetry, and a lingering sense of inferiority. "Say, did your fathers cross the dry

Sierras / To build another London? / Do Americans always have to be second-rate?"[3] This American attitude is sometimes matched by British insularity, snobbery, or toadying that conceals contempt. But, as we shall see, comparisons between the amount of good poetry written in Britain and America cannot always be so facilely made. At this writing, the ratio of the population of the United States to that of Great Britain is about 3.75 to 1. So although there appear to be many more American poets than British, this partly reflects the relative size of the populations. But even if we discount the chauvinistic self-aggrandizing of some poets, there still remain some very real areas of transatlantic misunderstanding. Donald Davie points out "that for many years now British poetry and American poetry haven't been on hearing terms."[4] The editor of the Oxford English Dictionary, Robert Burchfield, has gone so far as to say that in the future Britons and Americans will speak two separate languages. Against these predictions of division must be set the ever-increasing amount of inexpensive air travel between the two countries and the flood of television programs which familiarize ordinary people in each country with the other's idioms. (No British tot who watches *Sesame Street* is baffled when Oscar says he lives in a *garbage can* rather than in a *dustbin.*).

Many of the fundamental differences between contemporary American and British poetry arise from the contrasting sets of values which they use to judge new work. (These values are not necessarily mutually exclusive, but the British and Americans give them different priorities.) For Americans, the touchstone is innovation: Pound's dictum "Make it new" is invoked over every fresh (and sometimes desperate) attempt to depart from the poetic norm. Along with this reverence for innovation go an American emphasis on the practical and an attempt to reproduce present reality according to Williams's "No ideas but in things." But for the British the past—literary, political, historic and mythical—is inescapable, and British poets feel compelled to work out their relationships, positive or negative, to it. This British past does not mean only history, but also many poets who are still read, and in that sense, still alive. This long literary tradition also implies that new poetry is inevitably compared with the achievements of the past and that there is a set of standards which ought to be applied to new poetry. (In contrast, many American poets have vociferously rejected any standards for judging poetry.) The British handbook *Fowler's Modern*

English Usage concerns itself with what ought to be said; its counter-part, A *Dictionary of Modern American Usage*, "confines itself to what is; it is not concerned with what should be." The British poets' attempts to reconcile their present with their past, when they had more economic and political power, is similar in some ways to the Surrealists' attempts to integrate reality and dream. Their compelling tradition means that British poets must venture beyond the present into the past on what Charles Tomlinson has called "the voyage of recovery."[5] This is the direction in which the best British poets attempt to extend poetry's bounds.

The sense of privacy is another British trait which Americans often misunderstand. There seems to be more distance between British poets and their readers, just as privet hedges shield British gardens, unlike the rolling continuous lawns of American suburbia. The Britons' sense of privacy has both good and bad effects on their poetry. Certainly it goes against the confessional tendency of recent years and can make some British poets seem lackluster. Yet this lack of surface pyrotechnics can be deceptive: as we saw in Chapter Two, Larkin's fishbone lines and Enright's *bons mots* can stick in the memory long after the bleatings of Berryman have been forgotten. The British restraint sometimes prevents poets from being bold enough to have an individual flavor, and it is possible to read through certain anthologies without realizing the poems are by different poets. On the other hand, British restraint can be less intimidating and more inviting to the reader than the agonies of Extremism or the obscurities of Surrealism.

Another common misconception about Britain is that it is one homogenous country. In fact it is, and always has been, a conglomeration of regions, tribes and classes. Not only can Britons be placed in specific regions by their speech (which is also true of Americans), but they also reveal instantly their class through their pronunciation and choice of phrases (which is not so true of Americans.). These nuances of class and region mean that apparently subtle shifts in style can have a major significance. Because language has such social and cultural power, many Britons try to use it carefully and precisely. The middle-class intelligentsia who speak and write standard "Oxbridge" or BBC English oppose these diverse idioms of various classes and regions as provincial barbarities. Yet for all its apparent stability, the language of Britain has undergone many radical changes in the past and continues to do so. A variety of invaders long ago insured against linguistic insularity, as have the British traditions of sea voyages, empire-building and explorations.

One of the most thorough attempts to integrate the British past and present is Geoffrey Hill's *Mercian Hymns*. This sequence of thirty short poems in free verse traces the life of King Offa of Mercia (who reigned from 757 to 796 A.D.) from his coronation to his death-bed and outlines his achievements, such as coining a stable currency, writing a code of laws, building Offa's Dyke along the Welsh border and dealing with Charlemagne as an equal and a friend. Today much of the West Midlands where Offa reigned is a utilitarian and unromantic manufacturing area. Hill includes in Offa's list of titles such modern appellations as "overlord of the M5" (a superhighway) and "contractor to the desirable new estates."[6] In some ways, present-day England has declined since the Anglo-Saxon kingdom: battle-names have become quaint names given to cute cottages by their pretentious but "entrenched" owners. Hill, however, sees a continuity: "Steel against yew and privet. Fresh dynasties of smiths."[7] Because he does not romanticize the past, the ignobility of the present does not depress him. Hill's focus is on the past as history rather than as myth; although Offa is connected with the perennial Greene King of the holly groves, he is a figure moving from legend into history. The means by which he does this, his source of power, is the minting of a reliable currency rather than his mythic or tribal descent. Offa's head on his coins is "Coiffured and ageless, portrays the self-possession of his possession, cushioned on a legend."[8] Offa's coins, "handsome as Nero's," are also his immortality, and by extolling Offa's treasure Hill is also implying that it is wrought things (like art) which endure.

But minting and metal-working, particularly in modern industry, take a human toll:

> I speak this in memory of my grandmother, whose
> childhood and prime womanhood were spent in the
> nailer's darg.

> The nailshop stood back of the cottage, by the fold. It
> reeked stale metal sweat. Sparks had furred its low

roof. In dawn-light the troughed water floated a
damson-bloom of dust—

not to be shaken by posthumous clamour. It is one
thing to celebrate the "quick forge," another to cradle
a face hare-lipped by the searing wire.[9]

Offa is also, obliquely, Hill himself as he remembers his "rich and
desolate childhood. Dreamy, smug-faced, sick on outings—I who was
taken to be a king of some kind, a prodigy, a maimed one."[10]

Even the grimmest industrial scenes are illuminated by mystery
and splendor: "In tapestries, in dreams, they gathered, as it was en-
acted, the re-entry of transcendence into this sublunary world."[11] Hill
then describes the splendid English medieval embroidery, but almost
immediately miners appear: "They trudged out of the dark, scraping
their boots free from lime-splodges and phlegm. They munched cold
bacon."[12] In the last line miners and glowing tapestries are reconciled
and joined: "The lamps grew plump with oily reliable light."[13] There
is a strong religious element in Hill's poetry, sometimes expressed
through conventional Christianity; sometimes, as above, in a belief in
a transcendent splendor beyond our world.

The Mercian Hymns are formal and controlled in their tone (although they are free verse arranged in paragraphs rather than lines),
and Hill's plethora of scholarly notes and crossing of time barriers is
reminiscent of Eliot. Like Offa's coins, Hill's poems are small and
rare, but they are also a rich hoard of past and present that glows more
as we rub them again and again.

Ted Hughes is a poet who has attempted a deep exploration both of
his tradition and of his region. Although (with Larkin) he is probably
the best-known recent British poet, Hughes does not immediately fit
the stereotype of restrained British poet. In Britain, which has been
cultivated and civilized for centuries, Hughes finds his own wilderness
and savagery. He grew up in the West Riding of Yorkshire, near the
Brontës' home, and the elemental struggles of these lonely moors
seem to pervade Hughes's work. "The most impressive early companion of my childhood was a dark cliff . . . a wall of rock and steep
woods half-way up the sky, just cleared by the winter sun. This was

the *momento mundi* over my birth: my spiritual midwife at the time and my godfather ever since. . . . From my first day it watched. If it couldn't see me direct, a towering gloom over my pram, it watched me through a species of periscope: that is, by infiltrating the very light of my room with its particular shadow. . . . I lived under it as under the presence of a way, or an occupying army: it constricted life in some way, demanded and denied, and was not happy. Beneath it, the narrow valley, with its flooring of cricket pitch, meadows, bowling greens, streets, railways and mills, seemed damp, dark and dissatisfied. . . ."[14] This landscape, together with the proverbial Yorkshire stubbornness tinged with provincial spitefulness and pretentions, can make many of Hughes's poems as dismal as English winter drizzle. He has struggled throughout his life to escape the brooding rock (and all that it stands for) which overshadowed his childhood. In this conflict, Hughes is like D. H. Lawrence, who used sensuality in his fight to escape English provincialism.

A favorite theme of Hughes's is the metamorphosis of humans into animals as people's essential bestial natures assert themselves. In his early poems, animals are frequently hunted and imprisoned; in later poems, such as those in *Crow*, the demarcation line between man and beast has vanished. Hughes's animals, although realistically detailed, are not amoral as are natural animals. Very few animals, for instance, take pleasure in killing, but Hughes's animals are often sadistic. In "Crow and Mama": "He jumped into the rocket and its trajectory / Drilled clean through her heart he kept on."[15] Hughes's beasts, like the serpent in Eden, are as scheming and nasty as the worst humans. And also like the serpent in Eden, they have an element of the demonic in them. Hughes's latest book, *Gaudete*, goes a step further and shows a man possessed not merely by a malevolent animal, but by a demon.

This aspiration (or desperation) toward hell results from his deep and bitter disappointment with heaven. Hughes is not a typical atheist intellectual: he is enraged at God for apparently not existing or caring. Hughes taunts God as a gnat or a fool: "within seconds the new-born baby is lamenting / That it ever lived— / God is a good fellow, but His mother's against Him."[16] Yet like many mockers of God Hughes is unable to hurl his insults and stalk off; he loiters among the back pews, notably in *Gaudete*, which is about a parson possessed by demons who send his double out to seduce all the women in the parish. (This theme is dearly beloved, as witness the number of "the bishop said to the actress" jokes.)

Gaudete shows us where Hughes turned when Christianity failed him: to the ancient myths and fertility rites. The parson has been replaced by a Dionysus-like figure who transforms the respectable local women into frenzied Bacchantes. Because Hughes knows that fertility rites existed and that madness and sex exist, he finds them a more certain foundation for his poem than conventional religion or philosophy. When he attempts to harness the hidden life forces of the countryside to his poetry, Hughes goes beyond the niceties maintained by many British poets of the fifties. At the conclusion of *Gaudete,* the parson is slain by the cuckholded husbands but is resurrected in the West of Ireland as a strange man who gives three little girls a book of poems. Unfortunately the lyrics which end the book are too weak and diffuse to bring concord to Hughes's savage universe and to evoke the "rejoice" of the Latin title. And so we must ask if Hughes can really manufacture (or synthesize from old myths) a new myth compelling enough to structure an entire book. His personal conglomerations are not myths because he is not inclusive or tribal. (His children's stories and poems with invented "mythic" characters are quite effective; these characters function perfectly well in a fairy-tale context but are not credible enough for a full-scale cosmology.) It is as if Hughes presumes that his country folk make connections between fragments of myth which would have confounded Jung; as if Hughes imagined a farm laborer as a Minotaur with a pitch-fork in one hand and a first edition of *The Golden Bough* in the other. Hughes uses his myth to put the large amounts of sex and violence in his poems at a distance from both the poet and the reader. As sex and violence are repeated in poem after poem, we come to expect them and they seem less shocking and more remote. So Hughes, supposedly the wild man of contemporary British poetry, still suffers from the tendencies toward over-intellectualization and distance from the reader which afflict other British poets.

Hughes's attempt to create a religious mythology also explains his tone of command and authority. Often he will repeat a word, or a questioning phrase, as if his poem were a kind of litany. (This technique is similar to that used by the American poet of the twenties Vachel Lindsay.) Another favorite device of Hughes's is bursts of alliteration, such as link together the lines of Anglo-Saxon poetry and

are found in Gerard Manley Hopkins. Yet often Hughes's long lines
and prose passages seem to have no inner music that molds them to a
certain shape, and they are sometimes marred by clichés such as "a
leaden sky." The apparatus of myth can be cumbersome and intrudes
on the poem's own unique reality. Shocking images are Hughes's
main tactic for jolting the reader, yet this effect diminishes with each
re-reading. Technically, and in his choice of themes, Hughes has not
opened any paths which younger poets have followed with success.
His shocking visions and imperative certainty, compared to the timid
equivocations of the fifties poets, helped to establish his reputation in
the early sixties. Yet the price he pays for this absolute and apocalyptic
tone is a loss of subtleties and ambiguities—Crow is black, black,
black, etc. If "man is walking abattoir" then there is no hope of
change to give a poem drama and conflict. [17]

In *Gaudete* Hughes's protagonist does try to "rejoice," despite the
irrational horror which has befallen him. And now perhaps Hughes
himself, after years of bleak, nihilistic poems and personal tragedy, is
trying to crawl out from under the shadow of the gloomy rock of his
childhood, from under the mood that gave his poems startling force in
the past but which has now become predictable.

Peter Redgrove's voyage of recovery is to a destination further back
than myth: he strives to discover the elusive threshold between life and
death. His search is primarily located in the natural world, acutely ob-
served, rather than in specifically British history. There is, however, a
strong English tradition of nature study (Darwin, Gilbert White, etc.),
and Redgrove held two scholarships in natural sciences at Cambridge.
His scientific training is evident in many poems that display rich detail
and reward his patient focus on a single subject.

> With its gleaming foot and coil of lime
> The snail emblazons a panting path
> Nerves wounded with eyes and afire with time
> Through the sun that would drink to death
> Its curling cup, to the wet shade
> And coronet of eggs, since the crown it has made
> Is new beginnings. . . . [18]

If poetry and science co-exist in Redgrove's intellect, science and obsolete tradition or even superstition co-exist in his poetry. In this he typifies a country where fellows of the older universities may do research with nuclear reactors by day, then dine in medieval gowns in medieval halls by night. Despite his scientific background, Redgrove's later poems are full of references to magic and conjuring. *Dr. Faust's Sea-Spiral Spirit* describes a wizard: "I utter the words of vertigo, were I so strong / I should vomit as I spoke them. . . . The great book opens of its own accord / Its snow-light floods the room, it comes, it comes, / The past has ripped away, there is a thin snow curling."[19] Ghosts frequently and convincingly haunt many of Redgrove's early poems, such as "Corposant":

A ghost of a mouldy larder is one thing: whiskery bread,
Green threads, jet dots,
Milk scabbed, the bottles choked with wool,
Shrouded cheese, ebony eggs, soft tomatoes
Cascading through their splits,
Whitewashed all around, a chalky smell,
And these parts steam their breath. The other thing
Is that to it comes the woman walking backwards
With her empty lamp playing through the empty house,
Her light sliding through her steaming breath in prayer.[20]

This menacing and morbid tone is found in a number of Redgrove's poems; these ghosts query the veil between the living and the dead and evoke a number of metaphysical poems.

Redgrove does not deal with death and other issues in the abstract, but in the context of very concrete human situations, like that of the widow in "The Patient Successor": "How the conversation would snap! / Now out of mourning she lies in her frock / Upon her like a shriek, and the long knives / Of rainbow colour clash to a peak. We could talk / But there's the fall of the snow, and wind pulls / Its bent shapes beneath, and below / Glassed in mud, abominably frozen, he."[21] The details of the predicaments in Redgrove's poems give them an urgency and a reality which is difficult for the reader to ignore. Redgrove does not sentimentalize nature and its decay (or love and its decay), yet he is basically affirmative and optimistic without being mawkish. In this he differs from Hughes, who gives negative answers to similar questions. Some of Redgrove's more wry human portraits, such as "Office Poems," are reminiscent of Larkin and Enright.

Redgrove's journey across the boundaries between death and life lead him to a kind of surrealism, particularly in his later poems where he expands his metaphors with great effectiveness. But it must be remembered that Redgrove has arrived at the surrealism in his poems by a logical progression from his subject matter, rather than by committment to an ideology derived from the visual arts, as did some other poets.

Redgrove has a flair for using just the right number of rare and unusual words to give his poems interest and an individual texture without being pedantic. Frequently he returns to the same subject in several poems, as if he were taking snapshots from several different angles, determined to get it right. (A parodist would probably do a Redgrove poem about one of his recurring topics, such as being caught in the rain.) Unfortunately, there are also some sloppy repetitions, and a real problem of loss of intensity in some long poems. The dramatic progressions and conclusions of his weaker poems don't seem inevitable, and some of their endings and beginnings might be re-arranged without being noticed. At his best, however, Redgrove is one of the most vigorous and fascinating contemporary British poets, conjuring large charges from still subjects, like the static electricity he has written about.

Charles Tomlinson is unusual among present-day British poets in that he is also a painter and graphic artist. His early poems, like some of his drawings, are precise attempts to record the exact details of objects and landscapes. In "A Garland for Thomas Eakins" Tomlinson speaks of "the stubborn / anguish of / those eyes" and describes Eakins struggling with the problems of anatomy, perspective and reflection by posing a model against a grid. [22] The landscapes which dominate Tomlinson's early poems are open but lush in detail, as if he were attempting to go beyond the bounds of superficial reality by a kind of hyper-realism. In this he shows the influence of Williams, which has not been widely felt in British poetry.

Yet landscape alone is not enough, and in his second book, significantly titled A *Peopled Landscape*, Tomlinson addresses an English widow farmer:

> For we who write
>   the verse you do not read
>   already plead your cause. . . .
>   Our language is our land
>   that we'll
> not waste or sell
>   against a promised mess
>   of pottage that we may not taste.[23]

Language is an inheritance, like land, to be cherished and husbanded. The people who now appear in Tomlinson's poems are also carefully drawn and indigenous to their landscapes. There is a distance between Tomlinson and his subject and between both and the reader.

Like other British poets, Tomlinson strives to come to terms with his tradition and the realities of contemporary Britain, "Too desolate, diminished and too tame / To be the foundation for anything."[24] There is a real conflict between the necessity for people to earn their livings and the ugly slag heap landscape left by the industrial revolution. Tomlinson offers no easy, fashionable answers, but seeks both to accept and to transcend the industrial reality with all its unappealing details by drawing them in. Landscape is not only language but history: "This place, the first to seize on my heart and eye, / Has been their hornbook and their history."[25] Tomlinson's intention is clear: "I write to rescue what is no longer there."[26] The history he wants to recover is the relatively recent experience of ordinary people, not the Mercian kings of Hill or the myths and rituals of Hughes. To a certain degree, Tomlinson is anti-Romantic and prefers landscape to legend. "But who won, or what gods / Saved the bare appearances of it all / Is written in no history. / Their pantheon was less powerful than this wall."[27] He is also rebellious at times against English history and culture; he has been influenced not only by Williams but also by Stevens and has maintained contact with Black Mountain poets like Creeley. Tomlinson held a visiting professorship in New Mexico for a time, and this prompted a number of poems in *American Scenes*. Yet for all his involvement with America, he remains somewhat contemptous of places like Barstow: "Nervy with neons, the main drag / was all there was. A placeless place / A faint flavour of Mexico in the tacos / tasting of gasoline. Trucks refuelled / before taking off through space. . . ."[28]

Tomlinson's careful progression from landscape to figures in a landscape continues in his recent book *The Way In*, in which he includes his own portrait, as did medieval painters who added their own portraits to those of the subject and donor. Tomlinson has come to autobiography relatively late, yet with a force that suggests that all his work has been building toward self-revelation. In "The Marl Pits" not only does he reveal his own background, but in doing so he also reveals the source and intention of his language:

> It was a language of water, light and air
>   I sought—to speak myself free of a world
> Whose stoic lethargy seemed the one reply
>   To horizons and to streets that blocked them back
> In a monotone fume, a bloom of grey.
>   I found my speech. The years return me
> To tell of all that seasoned and imprisoned. . . .[29]

Language for Tomlinson is a tangible medium, like paint, which he uses to oppose vague inarticulate grayness.

Tomlinson's interest in recent history, which represents both stability and flux, is part of his wider interest in the process of change, which is the subject of many poems in *Written on Water*, such as "La Promenade de Protée": "Changing, he walks the changing avenue: / this blue and purple are the blue / and purple of autumn underwater. . . ."[30] And language itself, so fugitive, "of water, light and air," is nevertheless a vessel of stability which Tomlinson uses to make "the voyage of recovery."[31]

The steady, careful progression of Tomlinson's work is notable in these times when many poems feel that they must publish frequently and indiscriminately. Sometimes his subjects can seem too abstract and sparse; at other times his scruplousness seems over-cautious and pernickety. But Tomlinson is one of the few poets whose next book we can confidently expect to be richer and better written than his last.

Some British poets have to come to terms not only with their literary tradition but also with the cultures which characterize the various "principalities" within the United Kingdom: Wales, Scotland and Ulster are the major regions, but other areas also impart their particular flavor to their native poets. Provincial poets found more acceptance in the sixties and seventies than in the fifties, when the literary power centers were almost exclusively in London, Oxbridge and the BBC.

Welsh poetry written in English has gained strength: first in the late thirties with the publication of Dylan Thomas and others, and recently in the "second flowering" of the late sixties and the seventies. Before this "second flowering," Welsh poets writing in English had sought audiences (and, of necessity, publishers) in London. But the revival of the Welsh language and of Welsh nationalism has articulated a fierce regional pride and traditions. Indeed, many Welsh poets writing in English bristle at being labeled "Anglo-Welsh." Wales, of course, is renowned for its music, its singers, and, from prehistoric times, its bards, who have always been esteemed. One of the most important things which the English, and, even more, the Americans can learn from the Welsh is the natural position of the poet in Welsh society. Butchers, farmers, schoolmasters, and sailors may (and do) all write poetry, both in Welsh and in English; so a person may be a poet without being set apart as one of the elite, either by education or by birth. Nor does being a poet mean being a bohemian outcast—a role into which Americans often force their poets, and a role which they tragically encouraged in Dylan Thomas.

Recent Welsh poets have written in a variety of forms and textures. One of the most highly regarded is R. S. Thomas, whose first book was published in 1946. Like other British poets we have considered, he attempts to come to terms with a tradition, for "You cannot live in the present, / At least not in Wales. / There is the language for instance, / The soft consonants / Strange to the ear."[32] Only since 1901 have more Welsh people spoken only English rather than Welsh alone or both languages, and recently the Nationalists have encouraged bilingual signs, classes and even television programs. (Outsiders sometimes suspect that one of Wales's strongest defenses against invasion has been the tongue-twisting place names!) R. S. Thomas is rather caustic about the tourists who come to gawp at Wales as a quaint backwater:

> I have walked the shore
> For an hour and seen the English
> Scavenging among the remains
> Of our culture, covering the sand

> Like the tide and, with the roughness
> Of the tide, elbowing our language
> Into the grave that we have dug for it.[33]

R. S. Thomas is vicar of a small hill parish in Northern Wales, and some of his portraits appear as naturally as if he were making his rounds. Often he lets his hill farmers and hirelings speak for themselves in lyric monologues that echo Yeats's "Crazy Jane" poems. Thomas, however, has no romantic illusions about his parishioners: ". . . the hedge defines / The mind's limits; only the sky / Is boundless, and he never looks up. . . ."[34] While he is painfully realistic, he is not unsympathetic, and he is skilled at putting himself (and his readers) into the boots of his hard-luck smallholders.

The religious element in his poetry is expected but not obtrusive. He is also a realist (yet not an agnostic) about modern unbelief and the difficulties of belief. Many of the poems in *Frequencies*, one of his recent books, deal with the problems of belief, and some are addressed directly to God.

One of the most appealing traits of Thomas's poetry (which it shares with other Welsh poetry) is its relaxed cadence, which is inviting but not slack, musical yet sinewy. He is truly Welsh in his concerns and subjects, yet his poems have a wider relevance and appeal.

Scots poets who write in English face difficulties which resemble those encountered by Welsh poets. There is a native tongue, Scots Gaelic, as well as strong regional dialects which are almost incomprehensible to other Britons. Scotland also has a long line of poets: from the balladeers to Burns and others, and recently Hugh MacDiarmid. This literary tradition, together with vigorous cultural and nationalistic movements, can become a tartan shroud around emerging poets, the best of whom struggle against becoming cultural clichés, yet draw their strength from their heritage. They try to write colorfully, yet unaffectedly, and to capture pugnacity without being strident. The poetry readings which were popular in the sixties encouraged some Scots poets to do dialect poems, which seem more natural when spoken than when written. Poetry in Scots Gaelic has also continued strongly, but without the misty Romanticism of the Victorians' "tartanomania." The Scots today, always realists, now have new-found muscle through

Nationalist members of Parliament (who, for a time, held the balance of power through coalitions with the Labour government) and through the economic boom brought by North Sea oil.

Edwin Morgan was born in Glasgow and still teaches there. Some of his poems show Glasgow at its roughest, with its slums, chronic jobless, derelicts and alcoholics. "Meth-men mutter on benches, / pawed by river fog. Monteith Row / sweats coldly, crumbles, dies / slowly. All shadows are alive."[35] Although sympathetic with his down-and-outs, Morgan is unsparing of the unsavory details of their existence in urban areas. At the same time he acknowledges the occasional exuberance of Glaswegians in poems such as "Trio," about two laughing girls and a boy at Christmas time: "The chihuahua has a tiny Royal Stewart tartan coat like a teapot-holder, / the baby in its white shawl is all bright eyes and mouth like favours in a fresh sweet cake, / the guitar swells out under its milky plastic cover, tied at the neck with silver tinsel tape and a brisk sprig of mistletoe. . . ."[36]

Morgan's wide range of subjects and styles is a result of his idea of the purpose of poetry: "I think of poetry as an instrument of exploration, like a spaceship, into new fields of feeling or experience (or old fields which become new in new contexts or environments). . . ."[37] Morgan has done many translations from Anglo-Saxon, Russian, Italian and French. He is one of the few poets, British or American, to have written seriously about space exploration. This does not preclude his poking fun at some of the more comic sides of space travel. In "The First Men on Mercury" astronauts encounter natives speaking gibberish (which sounds suspiciously like drunken Glaswegian on Hogmanay, the Scots New Year's Eve revels); by the end of the poem the natives are speaking English and the astronauts gibberish. This wit, cannyness, and willingness to say the emperor has a bare backside characterize many Scots poets.

Voice is important to Morgan, both in dialect and in spoken poetry. In this he has acknowledged the influence of the Black Mountain poets, although he is not dogmatic about breath breaks, and his lines assume their own natural shape. He has also done Concrete poems, some of which are completely visual and only viable on the page; others, such as the sequence "The Horseman's Word," must be spoken aloud.

Edwin Morgan is one of the more adventurous British poets: he doesn't always succeed, but he explores divergent paths. He is intensely local, but not parochial; he has the common touch but is not anti-intellectual.

Ulster has an even more complicated heritage than Wales or Scotland, and its problems have recently appeared all too often on our television screens and in our newspapers. At the same time, industrial expansion has increased, universities have expanded and the arts have been encouraged. A number of Ulster poets have appeared, among them Seamus Heaney, who was raised on a farm in County Derry. He often writes about the basic acts of rural life, in poems which use detail precisely, strongly and naturally. (Irish poets of the "Celtic Twilight" would not have dared to write about such commonplace subjects as digging potatoes for fear of being thought "stage Irish.")

Heaney shares with other poets in this chapter a voyage of recovery. He speaks of "my need / for antediluvian lore" and sometimes writes about the bodies and other remains of prehistoric peoples found in peat bogs.[38] Ancient customs persist into our times; "The Last Mummer" still appears and has seasonal power even though the family is now charmed by the television screen. Yet like his farm poems, where "living displaces false sentiments," Heaney's poems about prehistoric times are not excessively romantic.[39] He says to Tolland Man, excavated from a Danish bog: "In the old man-killing parishes / I will feel lost, / Unhappy and at home."[40]

No Ulster poet can escape the recent political troubles:

> This morning from a dewy motorway
> I saw the new camp for the internees:
> A bomb had left a crater of fresh clay
> In the roadside, and over in the trees
>
> Machine-gun posts defined a real stockade.
> There was that white mist you get on a low ground
> And it was déjà-vu, some film made
> Of Stalag 17, a bad dream with no sound.
>
> Is there a life before death? That's chalked up
> In Ballymurphy. Competence with pain,
> Coherent miseries, a bite and sup,
> We hug our little destiny again.[41]

Heaney, unlike some propagandists, does not specify the religion of the internees, and the implication is that here is one of the camps where both sides are imprisoned. In "Summer 1969" Heaney describes "two berserks club each other to death / For honour's sake, greaved in a bog and sinking."[42] Although he records the bombs and bluster of both sides, the poet's position is different: "I am neither internee nor informer; / An inner émigré, grown long-haired / And thoughtful. . . ."[43]

The Ulster poets' problems of relationship to the English politically extend to the English language. "Ulster was British, but with no rights on / The English lyric. . . ."[44] "Our guttural muse / was bulled long ago / by the alliterative tradition."[45] Nevertheless Heaney shows in his writing that he has a better command of the language than many English poets, and shares with other British poets an extreme caution with words because they can be so powerful.

> Northern reticence, the tight gag of place
> And times: yes, yes. Of the "wee six" I sing
> Where to be saved you only must save face
> And whatever you say, you say nothing.
>
> Smoke-signals are loud-mouthed compared with us:
> Manoeuvrings to find out name and school,
> Subtle discrimination by addresses
> With hardly an exception to the rule
>
> That Norman, Ken and Sidney signalled Prod
> And Seamus (call me Sean) was sure-fire Pape.
> O land of password, handgrip, wink and nod,
> Of open minds as open as a trap. . . .[46]

Sometimes this seemed to inhibit Heaney's early work, whose excellent description was not always sustained enough; latterly he has partly counteracted this tendency by writing longer sequences of short poems. Heaney has managed to transform the burdens of the past, contemporary political strife and the English language into vivid and memorable poems.

In the early sixties three significant approaches to poetry appeared as alternatives to the Movement attitudes which had prevailed in Britain during the fifties. First to become evident were certain poets known as "The Group," who found their main platform in *The Review* magazine, which was published from 1962 until 1979. Its editor, Ian Hamilton, writes poems which are typical of the *Review* style: short, inoffensive and pleasant lyrics which take no great risks with emotion or language. Yet in these poems he also shows a keen eye, intelligence and a determination not to settle for second-best.

A second, and more interesting, alternative to Movement poetry is represented by the work of A. Alvarez. His influential anthology *The New Poetry* advocated Extremism and placed Lowell and Berryman in the front rank. Although Extremism was misunderstood to hold that *only* suicide and genocide were suitable topics for contemporary poetry, still the idea did seem to open new areas of experience which had been closed by British reticence for some poets. Alvarez's own poems are finely balanced between emotion and intellect. Humans are the landscape, rather than figures drawn against a landscape, and their emotions fuel the poems' movement on an intimate yet powerful scale:

> Abruptly, the smell of flowers, sharp, far, delicate,
> The old heart beating sweetly, eyes
> Fresh as an apple, all the wrinkles gone.
> Who would have thought it? Not her, not him. . . .
>
> "Hawthorn," he said, "mayflower, the late smell of
>   spring.
> Everything's opening up, just like it was.
> Won't you come with me?" he said. "We've still
> Got a chance. Listen. Smell it," he said,
> "We've been reprieved." Slowly, idly,
> She shook her heavy head and turned away.
> "I won't be waiting," she said. "Don't think I will." [47]

Alvarez's voyage of recovery is sometimes towards an old love, which leads him to the wider theme of absence and, ultimately, death. There are few British poets who have tackled the subject of death as boldly as Alvarez without being either distantly ironic or hysterical: his calmness and candor are reminiscent of Donne. In fact, Alvarez does not readily fit into the Extremist camp at all: his poems about domestic misery, for example, are more similar to Redgrove's than to Lowell's. Is his restraint a result of being a critic? Or perhaps it is because, despite his dislike of "gentility," he is, after all, English. Although his poems are not flashy, he has a command of the lyric and longer sequence and an excellent ear.

The third category of poets who attempted innovations in British poetry at this time were those influenced by the Black Mountain poets and by Basil Bunting, Like Olson, Bunting was influential as a rallying figure for younger discontents and a counterweight to establishment poets, rather than directly through his verse. Although some poets make extravagant claims for Bunting's genius, his verse can be synthesized by reading alternately a line of the late *Cantos*, then a line of Swinburne at his plummiest. Perhaps the best representative of this group is Roy Fisher. He was formerly a jazz musician, and jazz's method of improvisation has left its mark on his poetry, as has jazz's urban subject matter. Birmingham is Fisher's raw material, which he heats, hammers and shapes like the blacksmiths who forged the city's prosperity. "At crossings I could see people made of straws, rags, cartons, the stuffing of burst cushions, kitchen refuse. Outside the Grand Hotel, a long-boned carrot-haired girl with glasses, loping along, and with strips of bright colour, rich, silky green and blue, in her soft clothes. For a person made of such scraps she was beautiful."[48] These urban transformations are made possible by the force of the past. "In the century that has passed since this city has become great, it has twice laid itself out in the shape of a wheel. The ghost of the older one still lies among the spokes of the new. . . ."[49] Although Fisher appears different from other British poets in his techniques, he is also engaged on a voyage of recovery. The time he attempts to recover is often the moment before last, day before yesterday, "the ghost of a paper bag." Sometimes his work is limited and rather prosy, but his engagement with urban reality and his adaptation of Black Mountain techniques represent a significant direction in British poetry.

Meanwhile the "establishment" of poetry, like all other British institutions, prospers by appearing flexible to those who clamor for change, and a bulwark of stability to those who want the British literary tradition upheld. For example, in June 1976 the poetry establishment clashed with other poets who had radically different ideas about the future of British poetry in what became known as "The Punch-up at the

Poetry Society." This staid institution had ambled along quietly for decades until the sixties, when it was taken over (largely by default) by
poets who used it as a venue for experiments in Sound Poetry, Concrete Poetry, etc., and who were influenced by Americans and Surrealists. A bronze bust of Basil Bunting glimmered on the mantlepiece
under poster-poems. But by 1976 there were numerous dissenting
groups, each accusing the others of intolerance, ignorance, and so
forth: one faction demanded a return to rhymed verse, the DaDaists
disrupted meetings, other poets presented themselves as "moderates"
and held key publishing and reviewing positions. Whatever the aesthetic issues at stake, these groups often cohered on the basis of age,
personality, nationality, or method of writing. This fracas brought the
Poetry Society more publicity than it had had for years, some new
members, and an open discussion of issues affecting British poetry.
What does seem strange is the unspoken assumption that there should
be *one* center and one kind of poetry. (Perhaps this is a reflection of
Britain's system of constitutional monarchy: one ruler appoints one
poet laureate; both reign for life. Judging by the present poet laureate's
performance, Her Majesty might be well advised to keep a string of
poets in training in case one goes lame, just as she so successfully does
with her racehorses.) The dust has since settled at the Poetry Society
with no great victories for any faction (except, perhaps, the nebulous
establishment) and without any miraculous formulas appearing for a
poetry renaissance.

The difficulties faced by recent British poets are very much indigenous problems of tradition and temperament which cannot be instantly solved by transatlantic or European panaceas such as sound poetry or Surrealism (which becomes another device for putting distance
between the poet and the reader). Any answers will probably be found
within British poets' relation to tradition, in the voyage of recovery
which the poets in this chapter have embarked upon. While British
poets have not set the pace in the last thirty years, their roots in the
past have kept them from bending to every breeze of current fashion.
This relationship to the past does not mean total preoccupation with
it, or that the past cannot also relate to the contemporary world. A delicate balance must be sought between experiment and excellence
within a context of tradition, and this is by no means an exclusively
British problem. In a recent debate about the current state of British
poetry in the House of Lords (where else does the upper legislative

body discuss poetry seriously and sympathetically?), it was said that it was going through a rather lean period. This is the widely held picture of British poetry, and it was true about 1960. Yet there have been some quiet changes over the last twenty years, and the poets in this chapter demonstrate that while there is not one over-towering figure who is universally labeled "great," there are a significant number of mature poets doing work of interest and strength.

9

"We Say, Today. This Day": New Poets

Searching for new poets is the most exhilarating yet exhausting of literary adventures. It requires the dogged dementia of a gold prospector and the pathological optimism of a compulsive gambler. The sheer amount of poetry published in recent years is daunting enough; in addition, there is the confused aftermath of the collapse of faith in literary criticism. In other times, whether a work was good poetry was determined by how the words conformed to set verse patterns, conventional subject matter or critical concepts. Now whether work is poetry may be decided by its writer in isolation, saying: "I am a poet, therefore what I write must be poetry and I must cover a certain number of pages with it to justify my existence." Small wonder that the sixties and the seventies, the "please yourself" decade, have left almost more poets than readers. We have become so awed by esoteric experiment that most people are frightened to admit, "I've read this poem several times, checked out its references and read the critics' comments, but I still don't understand it, much less like it." Fair enough. Maybe the poem is not very good, or perhaps if you return to it after several years it might become clearer. Good poems, especially contemporary ones, are not always easy to read. (Which is not to say that if a poem is inscrutable it is, *ipso facto*, good!) Not only may language be used in an unfamiliar way, but the poem may move by jumps of surreal associations rather than as a narrative in a logical sequence. Painful subject matter may make new poems hard to read. Yet despite these problems the best new poems have a cockleburr tenacity that makes them stick to us and us to them until we understand them.

The touchstone question which we must ask when judging a poem is: "Does this poem intensify and widen our awareness?" We cannot rely on any particular style alone to do this: certainly the different groups discussed in the previous chapters have demonstrated that there is not just one way to write good poetry. Now these schools have begun to change, merge or split, and cross-breeding is evident in many newer poets. Nor is youth alone a guarantee of merit or even innovation. The adjectives, such as "new," "modern," "contemporary," which we use to describe recent poetry all refer to present time, yet we are seeking poems which will outlast a particular moment.

Poets establish reputations through various combinations of good poems, persistence and luck. As in other fields, people can become well-known by unsavory methods such as toadying to the famous, or touting as a major opus a flimsy pamphlet containing a few poems, or launching a blitzkrieg of readings anywhere and everywhere. Time and astute readers will sort out the "poeticians" without merit from poets of quality (who may also be opportunists). Yet despite the hucksters good new poets keep appearing in significant numbers. The eight poets we are about to look at are certainly not the only good, lesser-known poets writing today. My selection has had to be limited by space, time and chance. (For instance, if it had been sleeting one particular day, if my feet had hurt more, if the Algonquin Hotel in New York hadn't looked after my luggage, then I might not have chanced to ferret out one of these poets at yet another obscure bookstore.) When I was looking for new poets, I did not start with any age limits, nor did I use a quota aiming at a representative selection by sex, geographical origin, race or any other biographical factor. As it happened, these poets' backgrounds are quite diverse, and I have arranged their poems in order to stress their variety, not necessarily to indicate my preference. What these eight poets do have in common is an outstanding ability to take our imagination beyond its previous limits, now and hopefully for many years to come.

Jordan Smith's poems carry a stage further the recent tendency for metaphors to be extended. Details and textures such as "the dim tracks cobwebs leave on stone, / grey weathered into a fainter grey" enrich his work.[1] These images do not remain static pictures, however: in "Daguerrotype" an old woman's letter is "pressed in the diary / until its violet ink has blended with the black / phases of the moon. . . ."[2] In a similar way, Smith's metaphors merge, each extending the borders of the others, like figures in a watercolor. It would be easy for these diffused images to become weak, but Smith strengthens them by making them very specific and memorable and by carefully repeating them throughout a poem so that they form a latticework. This trellis of images supports the growth of complex emotions and ideas as stout poles support heavy grapevines. Smith's extension of metaphor is natural and is not done in a gimmicky, "literary" or self-consciously surreal manner.

Jordan Smith was born in Rochester in 1954 and was raised in upstate New York, whose rural landscape plays a large part in many of his poems. He has a good eye for local scenes: "Fishers, Mendon, Clinton, / The good bars are all hidden / In these one gas pump towns: / Groceries, oil, rebuilt transmissions."[3] Smith's landscape is not a blissful country scene but "land poor as the farmers who sell / or go broke while the suburbs rise with the taxes."[4] As the shopping plazas spread, Smith laments the loss of the isolated countryside he knew, although he is aware that while it is good vineyard land it can also break a man:

> . . . the old man
> is sick again, and the farm up for sale.
>
> All you remember is the trellis of moonlight
> over his face. He abandoned the fences
> as the fields grew more difficult, empty as a house
> without a single vase, or what a vase can hold.
> Ash. The veins of each leaf
> giving up their vintage at last, simply and in flame.
> You put your hand on my shoulder, say it's past
> time to thin the vineyard down. And we go out
> where the firs reel like a farmer gone
> half blind from his glass of bad whiskey. . . .[5]

Like Charles Tomlinson, Smith sees a close relation between people and their landscape: "I make this landscape / out of us."[6]

Inheritance, both from family and from the land, is a major concern of Smith's. In particular, he struggles with a very complicated kinship to his father. In "Sugar in the Gourd," Smith tries to readjust to his father, who has undergone electric shock treatment:

> . . . your mourning
>
> lasted years. Even now, you brood
> over old photographs, and your eyes
> are empty. Your words seem badly glued
> together, a puzzle of half-lies,
>
> half-truths, like a jigsaw left
> to warp in the rain. . . .
>
> You stare toward me
> often now, and still I'm sure I lost
> you on that doctor's table. Your knees
> jerked to kick me off.
>
> I hang on. You hang on. All these years
> later, you'd think we'd both forget.[7]

Smith's skill and nerve are evident in this poem where he deals with a painful subject without flinching, sensationalism or self-pity. This poem is followed by a series of poems after the paintings of Edvard Munch, which are used as departure points for Smith's personal struggle to confront a poisonous inheritance in which "we damn the living and love the dead."[8]

The final poem in his book, "The Oxbow," referring to an arm of the Erie Canal, beautifully harmonizes Smith's relationship both to his father and to his landscape. This poem drifts like a boat with its oars up, yet the backwaters it glides over reflect and focus all of Smith's previous concerns. "The Oxbow" begins obliquely, describing a shadowy mark on the rose-printed wallpaper of an empty house:

> Like the stain on the wall, on the patterned
> wallpaper. The way the shadows take
> my face and carry it through the roses,
> chains of roses and their soft dark.
> As if in an empty house the whiskey

> still drifted because a bottle was cracked years ago
> against the plaster. Because an old feud
> gives up at last on its quarrel, on anything
> but the mark it leaves.

It is autumn, and the house's windowpanes are broken, yet it is welcoming. "A poverty that tells us gently / we can always come back." The canal runs beside the house and under its porch, so close that boats rub its pilings, reminding Smith of a past incident: "When I broke the saltshaker / splinters of silver and glass, waves of salt, / grazed the dark floor." Banks of reeds are nearby, and a willow branch appears to dance, but disappears instead. The poet wonders:

> . . . Suppose one autumn morning on the towpath
> you saw a man vanish. The amber light, his song,
> then just leaves and dust. The pheasants rustling.
> Suppose this happens again and again,
> and you never catch up.

This sense of emptiness is echoed in the imminent winter, yet there remains

> The gash in the screen that invites us
> to a house that has always been there. Worn
>
> and familiar. Swaying in the mist. The island
> my father gave me as we drifted on a mountain lake.
> Through the window I watched him lift
> a blue clay bowl to the light, and set it back
> on the dark planks. No one has lived here
> for years. No one has left. The Oxbow,
> where the canal dead ends and swings back
> on itself under our porch.

The coming ice is strangely welcome, and is awaited. "A woman / who leaves the coffee on the stove and stares / at her face in the window to see her husband / come out of the snow." There is a need to take on another warmth, not only against the snow, but against a longer cold:

We've watched our bodies drift away
as the skiff breaks the thin ice along the shore.
The oars stroking are the first time
I ever thought of death. Suppose my face
was swept out of my father's hands, while he stood
among the roses and laughed.

The empty boat drifts away, leaving us on an island whose landscape
is our own reflections.

In this house

The light yellows. Even more slowly than autumn.
The peeling walls throw out a darkness
like a barge running its load of coal
all night through black water. You filled
a blue basin from the canal, and our faces
floating in it were the same. The only kiss
I ever gave myself. Because we were children
together. Because one day on the canal bank
you shot a muskrat. And now it drifts

Almost out of sight. A soft stain
that washes through brown leaves, green water.
A sheaf of old newspapers where the coffee
spilled and washed the faces almost away.
I stuff them in the window to keep out cold, take them out
always a little before spring. And see,
where the mug rested, there is the slow curve of the Oxbow,
and the wash of its backwaters under my hand.[9]

Smith's images and metaphors merge and repeat in a quiet and subtle flow. The whiskey stain on the wallpaper in stanza one is re-echoed in stanza ten as the darkness like a barge of coal thrown out by the peeling walls, then reappears as a drifting dead muskrat—"A soft stain"—in stanzas ten to eleven, and finally becomes a coffee stain on the faces in the old newspapers in the last stanza. These primary images then branch out into secondary ones: the broken whiskey bottle becomes a broken saltshaker and a gash in the screen. Secondary images may return to primary images as the bargeload of coal brings to mind the boats and canal throughout the poem.

Now that "The Oxbow" has resolved Smith's relation to his father and to his landscape, and introduced the new theme of his own death, he might move on to wider subjects, although the landscape of upstate New York may well dominate his work for some time to come. Jordan Smith's poems are profound and real: they are exciting and tangible evidence that the search for new poets is well worthwhile.

Craig Raine has a strong, convincing style that made me say, even on the first reading, "Yes. This is genuine. I must include him." This boldness, which distinguishes Raine from other young British poets, comes from his audacious use of images to make his poems vivid and multifaceted. "Rain is when the earth is television." [10] His descriptions are precise but unfussy. Excessive details can make some of his poems rather static; yet, "In the end, the detail reaches out." [11] These details enable him not only to extend his metaphors, but also to concentrate them. Because he can capture an object with a few details, he can move from idea to idea very quickly and conjure incongruities. This startles us and makes us look more closely: suddenly we realize that incongruities have concealed similarities. Notice dogs: "Their feet are four-leafed clovers / that leave a jigsaw in the dust. / They grin like Yale keys and tease / us with joke-shop Niagara tongues." [12]

Raine's poems are not surreal, nor are they the result of automatic writing. The everyday (with a few exceptions) is not transported to a personal dream-world. Most of the time, his poems' accuracy of observation keeps them anchored to reality. Yet often they have a very peculiar atmosphere, which the reader first senses in the fusion of the natural and the mechanical. "At night, the switches stare / from every wall like flat-faced / barn-owls, and light ripens / the electric pear." [13] Sometimes very ordinary objects take on natural weaknesses; at other times, natural things suffer from the shortcomings of inanimate objects. "Autumn afflicts the failed machinery of ferns with rust." [14] The everyday is infected not only with the uncanny, but even with the insane, as is the fishing rod in "Down on the Funny Farm": "the twitchy rod has lost its thread / and gone to pieces, / so we keep it in a canvas jacket / with the tapes firmly tied." [15] There are fewer risks of sentimentality if you write about people in the guise of objects, and

one might call Raine's method the "ironizing" of both emotions and
objects. And he does effectively vault over our cynical defenses, so that
by the end of "Down on the Funny Farm" we feel sorry for what we
thoughtlessly break every day—an egg:

> But is it still a comedy of humours
> to be suddenly touched
>
> by the sight of a new-laid egg?
> To want to wipe away
>
> from this one smudged face
> the mucus and the excrement,
>
> so many final straws
> and the dirt of all dried tears? [16]

Not only do objects assume human feelings; they also undergo the
death that comes to all of us, and which we attempt to deny and
disguise, as we do the crematorium: "this poetic diction, / this building at the edge of town, / its elaborate architectural periphrasis / to
avoid calling a spade / a spade. . . ." [17] Often the focus shifts uneasily
between the general and the particular, as in "In the Mortuary." Here
a female cadaver lies without name or distinguishing marks, yet the
poem reveals her body in vivid focus and "Somewhere else, not here,
someone / knows her hair is parted wrongly / and cares about these
cobwebs / in the corners of her body." [18]

Raine's poems also flicker between being "funny" meaning odd
and being "funny" meaning amusing. Frequently they have a playful
tone, with whimsical puns and juxtapositions that at first may appear
as carefree as the toys dropped by a toddler. Yet the jaunty surface of
these poems is often a kind of nervous laughter concealing disturbing
implications. Raine has written several poems about his childhood, yet
he is not a directly autobiographical poet.

In the title poem of A Martian Sends a Postcard Home, the first
things the visitor from space describes are books:

> Caxtons are mechanical birds with many wings
> and some are treasured for their markings—
>
> they cause the eyes to melt
> or the body to shriek without pain.

I have never seen one fly, but
sometimes they perch on the hand.[19]

Raine has also discovered a world of books, first as a student and
teacher at Oxford and presently as the editor of *Quarto*, a new literary
magazine. In his poems there are some erudite references, but they
are not overwhelming. Now that Raine has accomplished a great deal
in his first two books, he must wrestle against his own natural strength,
the metaphor, to prevent it from becoming a mannerism. Raine's
achievement is to give us a fresh and even naive gaze at our world, to
make us recognize that we are all our own Martian invaders, even on
our home planet.

Lynn Strongin writes about pain and strength in a striking way. Certainly she is not typical of the soft-centered seventies, when the goal
was personal pleasure and self-fullfillment. Nor is she like the Extremist poets, who wrote almost exclusively about their own mental
anguish. She has said of her work that she wants to take risks and not
to insulate people.[20] Her mood is similar to that of a child with cancer
in one of her poems—"determined not angry"[21]—and this tone results
in poems that go right to our nerve endings because they are so finely
controlled. One of her major preoccupations has been to explore "the
relation between poetry and medicine" and she has been continually
sketching a portrait of a woman doctor which will culminate in a
novel, *Emma's Book*. In this concern with medicine, she resembles
the German poet Gottfried Benn; although her hospital scenes are not
as naturalistic as his, they are just as harrowing.

Go about living with the care of a diamond-cutter now.
Twilight, clinic closing
doors clang
silent.

Only emergency beds in the burn ward are open.
(Somewhere snow's blowing
fiercely in a little sawmill town.) . . .

Burnt-off touch
of a child's hand.
"Oh flesh, my small coat—taken."

Words
like ashes blew into my eyes.
Shipped back in this skiff of flesh.

Trembling, travelling.
They bring ammonia, one step shy of oxygen, the cruel-bright.

It's a long way from here
but don't lose consciousness—
moving fast, now my clear sight.[22]

The core experience (*core* in the sense of the rods in an atomic re-actor) which generates her poems about children in the hospital was her own illness with polio when she was twelve, which has left her permanently confined to a wheelchair. But her personal experience appears only obliquely in her poems. Her paradoxical combination of reticence and intensely personal, bone-aching events allows her poems to transcend her particular experience and refer to suffering in the widest sense.

Often mirrors appear in Strongin's poems, and they reflect not one, but a number of different *personae*, which represent a variety of human experiences. These transformations are extended in a sequence about Alice "through the looking glass" in *Nightmare of Mouse*. Be-cause of this multitude of identities, her later poems can, on first read-ing, seem obscure in a manner reminiscent of Robert Duncan's. Lynn Strongin was raised in New York and New England, lived in Califor-nia, and in 1971 moved to New Mexico, whose desert not only pro-vides the landscape for many of her poems, but also matches their tone: clear, flint-edged and vast in implication. She has an intense vi-sual sense, and light plays many roles, particularly in poems which could be "still-lifes" but are full of vibrant life. "My mother had courage to shove me out into the unknown. / I step out a blue door-frame / color of flame this grey morning: / have I the courage for this one?"[23]

She had some problems with style in early poems (some over-ob-vious and elaborate, some rhetorical), but in the mid-seventies her style changed dramatically, and her poems have a new simplicity and energy. This is evident in a group of love lyrics addressed to a young woman which alloy delicacy with power.

Neither by my poems nor your art will anyone ever be
quite able to explain our affair.
But it glows in sun (like the little hounds

released from hunt):
It is warm, it is here—
stretched out, relaxed by the fire.

You will rise at night
to brush back your monkish hair
and perhaps tone down the color of the girl's cheek

in the picture. I may temper my poem, not so tender.
But today I would have struck
the first aspen from earth to bring you in its original flame:

Passion—Has it any other name? [24]

When she was first at Hunter College, Strongin studied musical composition, then "found the transition very natural from music to poetry"
and continues in poetry her goal in music, "form expressing mood." [25]
She explores the musical possibilities more than many contemporary
poets and takes chances with internal rhymes, assonances and puns.

Underlying Strongin's poety is her conviction that the physical
world is an extension of the spiritual world, the Jewish mystical idea of
"as above, so below." This enables her not only to find the diamond-
like in the everyday, but also to transform hospital life without denying
its pain.

Adrenalin is the color
of the doctor's cheek in morning.
The girl in silver chair, foil wings

a bead of mercury
"The fever it is to be human"

measuring our
stamina.
Endurance is the color of the doctor's cheek
   in evening. [26]

It may be as disturbing to read Strongin's poems as it is to endure life at certain times. But because they confront and transcend life's bonds so boldly the reader feels a breathtaking sense of clarity and freedom.

The landscape of the Southwest also plays a large part in the poems of Rolly Kent, who has lived there for the past seven years and is presently Writer-in-Residence at Tucson Public Library. Kent uses his poems to reveal what is so deeply hidden that it is almost impossible to talk about. "It is a little like asking kids what a monster is, describe him. They never tell you about the ones that are real. They cannot describe those. A monster is a monster. But the monsters they speak of they have made. The truth is, there are two monsters. One is shaggy and skinned and has eyes and is blind and has fifteen arms and is yukky with bad breath and corns and ketchup all over, that's how terrible they are; the others, the others, you just keep quiet about and go under the covers and hope they'll never see you. The function of language is to find a way to consciousness."[27] Kent's use of "deep images" relates him to the American Interior poets. Yet despite his ambitious quest to make an inner vision comprehensible, Rolly Kent isn't solemn or overly cerebral. His poems are within our reach because of their relaxed cadences which are colloquial, yet strong and lean.

Time and memory bring to awareness emotions that are hard to articulate. In several poems about his family, Kent takes us vividly right into his world. A small boy, at home sick, listens to his dying grandmother recall her youth when she was the belle of the seaside and met his late grandfather:

> . . . The bed sailed through her voice,
> taking him to a room shrouded in a cold
> November fog of liniment.
>
> Someone was sifting sand through the curtains,
> Through pale circles of sun. A man in black,
> spinning in a yellow inner-tube, around
> and round. The waves were someplace else,
> but above his head silver spokes descended,
> flashing.

   "Weeeee!" Grandpa yelled, and kicked up
the water. "Weeeee!"
                    It was like a whistle almost,
spiralling down a pipe. Then he saw how
far away Grandpa was, and the dark
between them. Grandpa, the last thing
before invisible . . .[28]

As a child, Rolly Kent would sit in the kitchen listening to the adults
tell stories, and absorbed not so much the literal meaning of what they
said but the emotional atmosphere around him, which implied forces
larger than himself. Kent's poems often tell a story, but they have dis-
concerting time leaps that take them beyond simple narrative. Suddenly you realize that the poem's logical sequence and its carefully
built-up details are there to contrast abruptly with another hidden reality, just as the best ghost stories are so painstakingly logical in their
natural details that we believe any supernatural characters who may
appear.

   Space and landscape are additional means Kent uses to make the
abstract tangible. "Higher language starts with particular places," he
has said.[29] The Arizona desert is not only a backdrop or a mood in his
poems but a protagonist, as in "The Wreck in Post Office Canyon":

   From this rim you cannot see the river,
   but you hear it, swelling
   with snow and skull-sized boulders,
   the bastard logs that escaped the mill. . . .

   Mind floats disbodied in the gap,
   the stack of death-cards
   comes down at random:
   bottle of rum, blanket,
   dog-food, grocery bill, gum,
   arm in the scrub-oak, glass-bitten face,
   the zipper of blood . . .
   What is wrecked scatters,
   and you stare into all the arrangements.
   Any story ends.

   But something can happen
   even the telling of it cannot put an end to.

Here is the place
where the scream arched across
from one world into what? . . .

Not death, then, but this
bridge of attention
draws you here.
Something reaches out
as the sound of water is the sound of reaching,
and in that sound you are connected
to what cannot be said.[30]

In his poems Rolly Kent throws bridges of attention across various
canyons in our understanding. "The magic of poetry comes from its
ability to transform separateness into connectedness."[31] This striving
toward wholeness and his belief that it exists give many of Kent's
poems (particularly lyrics) an exuberance and contentment that make
them a pleasure to read. Sometimes he states plain truths too quickly
or flatly for them to have the impact they ought to have. The culmination of his endeavor to bring remote events within our understanding is the color blue, particularly as it appears in "For Friends,"
the final poem in his book *Blue House*.

The bluest evening drifts easily over hills,
seeping from the ground like dye
from the work-shirt, darkening the water.
And this blue! Such a blue it surely cannot last,
shimmering streams, currents of it,
an aura of the about-to-be, like a woman's hair
falling ahead of her into sleep . . .

Across the field of fenced desert the carpenters
are going home. The houses they are building
are dark, and the houses the sun built in canyons,
the blue house of the sky—blue
made from longing to be one thing!

We say,
Today. This day. But it is some day, and I am
far away across two deserts, calling you—

This blue light that took so long to speak
has come forward from the dark, like the echo
inside the thin iron of blackened bells: something
from the back of our lives comes forward,
it remembered and came back, taking us
by the hand, leading us where we already are—
The blue of morning. The blue of night.
Ending which touches the beginning,
as I reach out into the same blue, this blue
of everywhere.[32]

In Alex Gildzen's poetry, two main styles have developed parallel to each other. The more accessible style appears in three poem-journals, one of which, *The Yearbook*, spans the course of an entire year in 124 poems. Gildzen is very conscious of the act of writing itself and lets the reader look over his shoulder as he writes. Or, as the case may be, doesn't write: for he is quite candid about writing blocks. The epigraph to his first book of journal poems is his fellow poet Steve Osterlund's advice to try writing a poem a day for a month. Not only does this exercise serve to loosen his writing block, but the steady movement of the journal poems matches the passing of time, which Gildzen is acutely aware of. "Write a poem a day" also fits in with his early training as a *jour*nalist and his profession as a specialist librarian, documenting and cataloguing the letters of the famous. (When he searches out his birthplace, he finds the hospital has been turned into a library: "jesus   born in a library!" he exclaims in wry amazement.)[33] In addition to the need to record, Gildzen feels compelled to write in order to trace his own portrait in his fluid surroundings:

& how do i locate myself? alex gildzen
munching trappist cheese sent by the metcalfs
sitting at the round butcher-block-topped table in the kitchen
warhol's marilyn behind me
in front of me moore snoozing on the flokati rug
an hour ago i was in the purple-carpeted auditorium
of the new art building listening to harold rosenberg say
"technique is philosophy"
in 3 hours i will sit among strangers in the dark
watching "they only kill their masters." . . .[34]

From the flotsam and jetsam of everyday life, Gildzen fishes out souvenirs:

> & my desk begs permission to begin my biography
> I pause before the clutter
>> *una cabalgata* on Ira's postcard
>> Djuna Barnes peering thru a gold-edged oval
>> an unanswered 4-page letter from Paul
>> *Library Journal's* review of *The Origin of Oregano*
>> a stack of OCLC input work forms
>> the first issue of *Toucan* (Spring 1967)
>> an opened packet of Kleenex
> I see what will some day be my memorabilia [35]

This is a very personal poetry, often describing briefly people or events (sometimes only mentioning a name) which the general reader cannot be expected to recognize. The pitfalls here are obscurity and triviality, but Gildzen largely avoids them by effectively encapsulating someone in a few lines or by building up a cameo from repeated references to a character over the course of his journal books. What he achieves is an intriguing "moving picture" of extraordinary events in the course of an "ordinary" life: "so the year snails on / dragging its dead across pages / insisting I list the carrion / when what I really want to do / is break into 'The Leg of Mutton Rag.' " [36]

Death intrudes into Gildzen's *Yearbook*, not only the deaths of acquaintances and the famous, but the death of four students murdered in a demonstration at Kent State University in 1970. It is hard to imagine a more placid, out-of-the-way place than Kent State University, where Gildzen is an associate professor, yet the Vietnam war took its toll there also, and the student movements and hopes of the sixties ended on its campus that May morning. There was no such thing as a private life in times like those, and politics also intrude into Gildzen's "private" poems:

> the day began with cat feeding
> listening to a Rorem sonata
> as I prepared wheatgerm pancakes
> the radio announced that a singer
> at a White House reception last night

for the founders of *Reader's Digest*
stopped the show by asking
   "President Nixon, stop bombing
     human beings, animals and vegetation."
she blessed the Berrigans
& was asked to leave
the attorney general's wife said
   "She ought to be torn limb from limb."
then the station played "Bring Them All Back Home"[37]

This is an effective interweaving of the international and local which
shows how global events affect the individual. Sometimes the comparison is witty as well, as with the simultaneous state visits of Nixon to
Peking and Gildzen to his hometown:

Mother serves Charles blueberry cheese pie
it's cold but sunny in Elyria
& Dad has tried to explain electrical wiring to us. . . .

then the president arrives in Peking
where it's cold but sunny & people bicycle
wearing white masks over their mouths. . . .[38]

In our television age, every home is invaded by images of conflict.
News flashes flicker through Gildzen's journal poems, as do ghostly
memories of movie stars, which he finds more welcome. The journal
poems do not merely record private and public events in Gildzen's life:
they are a way of living through them: "I hug my friends / poets / sur-
vivors."[39]

    In addition to journal poems, Gildzen has developed a second
style by experimenting with a variety of forms beyond the conventional
poem on the page: prose poems, list poems, fiction, a poem for two
voices and dancers, envelope collages. "There are limitations to any
style. When I tired of free verse I composed a sonnet sequence. I don't
want holds on me can't stand bars UNLESS i put them up in front of
myself."[40] One of the most unusual of Gildzen's recent ventures is
Post Card Poems, thirty poems on card-sized sheets, each with a name
and address on the reverse, dated for each day in April and published
in an envelope. Some of these very brief, *haiku*-like poems are successful, but all too often they seem mannered and decorative. Here, as

in all new poetry, while experiments are to be welcomed, a poem is
not effective simply because it is experimental. Yet it is often poets like
Gildzen who venture beyond the conventions whose development is
most interesting to follow and who make the most refreshing discoveries.

Sometimes the fruits of experimentation will appear in poems
other than the ostensibly experimental ones. In Gildzen's work this is
true of a number of highly condensed short poems which are now
emerging in a third style. If his journal poems were reminiscent of
O'Hara, then these poems are closer to Ashbery's denser work. Gildzen's most recent book in this style is *New Notes*: while the images in
poems such as "The Search for Musk" are less deliberately autobiographical than in his journal poems, they still retain the strength of
personal details, and these new poems are more surreal, richer and
more muscular—all of which augur well for his future work.

> it's the hankering that drives us
> the memory of tongues
>
> in a room that remains the same. . . .
>
> . . . we snort the wet night
> grunting after the ox
> biting into flesh
>
> the taste of ourselves
> always shocks [41]

There is a conflict in Calvin Hernton's poetry between the need to
keep quiet and the need to speak out. In slavery days and long after,
the best tactic for many blacks has been: "Ah don't know nothin',
boss." Hernton, born in Tennessee, is well aware of this, not only in
the old-time South but as he sits in an English pub:

> From Third Avenue to Dalston Junction
> I cannot get a poem to function!
> Stoned without hope
> Sober without power—
> In London I have learned to expect
> What is to be expected. . . .

> Sit without being
> Be the absence of your presence
> Be nobody in a room of pale ghosts
> Perservering in fabricated dignity.[42]

Even in a fanatically unconventional commune dedicated to freaking out, Hernton alone feels the pressure to shut up in order to survive: "Stoned out of their minds drinking them- / Selves delirious looking for the atavistic / Gleam in their mother's eyes, and / Cursing America / All except one."[43] At the same time, Hernton's own experiences and the injustices blacks have suffered will not let him stay silent. He has written some of the most searing poems about the race riots of the sixties. Yet his poems, while passionate, are not one-sided propaganda: he tries to understand the mental states of such people as a slum landlord or even the terrorist who firebombed a church in Birmingham, Alabama, killing four children—"Hate is a bitter madness!"[44] Hernton is a sociologist by profession; he has written some well-known books on race relations as well as a novel and teaches Afro-American Studies at Oberlin College. He is driven by a need not only to record prejudice and to understand it, but also to express it in poetry, whatever the risks. "If I were your poet, America! / . . . You would hound me down, say I was / A mentally deranged Negro gone mad / Under stress of the civilized weight."[45]

Poetry is an almost magical ritual for Hernton, as it is for some other black poets. In the title poem of his book *Medicine Man*, Hernton tried to find his way back to African rituals:

> My knee bones hardening seven memories
> Recalled what I failed to know
> In an estranged familiar tongue. . . .
> But do not linger
> For the road back is never
> Home is never where you were born. . . .
> Hence I put away old handed-down ailments . . .
> And conjure Dance on pages of medicine book
>   of white hands[46]

Although he has written several ritual chants with an African setting, the magical chants most relevant to some of Hernton's poems are the "dozens," elaborate taunts which black kids shouted at each other. Handed down for a long time, these were first written down at the turn of the century and are often thought to be one basis for the blues. Usually a dozen contains some personal insults in the first line, incestuous insinuations in the second line and the revelation that "your mama don't wear no drawers" as a punch line. Hernton has written a hilarious dozen to the dozenth power (which is unfortunately too long to quote in full).

Your momma
Your momma's main man's momma
Fat momma, snagged-tooth momma, you girl friend's momma
Your momma's momma-in-law, incestuous momma
Liver-lip momma
Good loving momma, tender momma, boogalooing in the
        after-hours joint

Your momma's sister's daddy's uncle's momma's great-great-
        granddaddy's momma's momma, 13th century African tribe
        woman's momma
Ever-loving momma

High-yellow momma from the plantation tradition
Uncle Tom's momma, revolutionary momma, jive-ass momma. . . .

All!
Don't wear no draws.[47]

That's enough to knock the "draws" off any over-earnest ethnographer! Belief in the almost magical strength of words continues in Hernton's more serious poetry, as it does in classic blues: "If I could holler like a mountain jack / Go up on the mountain and call my baby back." As in much recent black poetry, Hernton emphasizes the word as spoken. "HOW YOU SOUND?? is what we recent fellows are up to," said Baraka (LeRoi Jones).[48] Hernton reads his own poems very well, and they are also effective on the page because, while he uses the blues' tone and commonplace phrases, his poems are not merely transcriptions of the blues, but take them into another dimension both of thought and of language. Just as the blues often conjure up a fantasy, then undercut it or mock it, so Hernton sometimes evokes a mood, then takes a step away from it into another kind of feeling.

As in the blues, people, their feelings and actions are paramount in Hernton's poetry. Many of his poems are portraits, many are autobiographical and almost all are dedicated to someone. What distinguishes Hernton's vision is that while his poems are unmistakably black, the scope of his imagination is wide enough to encompass almost anyone. In "The Gift Outraged" he wanders through Tompkins Square Park on New York's Lower East Side:

Many mornings
I have found myself in the park
Circled to circles
Where piss-stained benches call forth zombie
Supplicants pale and dry
From Buchenwald, Auschwitz, Dachau, Austria
The Ukraine—
And stray casualties
From where discarded wine bottles are of more value
Than human life—
All, huddled together still in concentration camped
Aggregates,
Sneer at me and mock me as I saunter among them
Forcing tears down my throat;
Not alone for my disillusionments
But for the gift outraged in the archaeological
Ruins of their faces. . . .

Evenings like these
I leave the park and prowl the Consolidated Edison streets
Where One finds his way to the agony of
Another's delicatessen.
And she, a serpent draped around her black thighs,
Stares the One down—
"Where are your eyes?" She harangues him.
"What happened to your arms?" She cries.
"What have you been doing with yourself all day?
Why don't you get a job? You have not kept your vows. . . .
Me and the child needs a husband, a home. *What's*
That damn fish doing in your hair! Why don't you answer me?
Answer me!"

> But the One stands there, dumb, shoulders
> Drooped over,
> Stripped of desire, drained of hunger,
> Forcing the dagger back down his throat;
> He knows as well as I that he is alone in the dark park
> Except for the revolving light in the big square clock
> Where the outrage is calculated,
> And the moon mumbles Black Sonofabitch at him
> Like that crocodile there, that hairy one on the barstool
> With the mean, smoldering eyes.[49]

That's strong medicine—very magical, very intelligent and very real. Long may Hernton's hoodoos be heard.

In Katha Pollitt's work there is a continual counterpoint between romance and disillusionment, between transcendence and skepticism. In the fourth of "Five Poems on Japanese Paintings," "Moon and Flowering Plum," she reveals this dilemma:

> A huge moon rises behind branches
> stippled with white plum flowers, cold and frail,
> like snow in early spring. Suddenly
> it is that moment you have longed for,
> you overflow like a cup,
> like the moon overflowing with whiteness.
> Could you live like that,
> moving from incandescence to incandescence
> as courtly viewers of plum flowers
> proceed from one white orchard to the next?
> Or would you find
> their formal robes too stiff, the moon too slow,
> the orchards, when you reached them,
> muddy and full of frogs?[50]

This is not Katha Pollitt's quandary alone but the mood of many poets as the eighties begin: they're not as optimistic as in the romantic sixties ("ya can do anything if your head is right"), but neither are they as cynical and detached as were the academic poets of the fifties. Katha Pollitt's reversals are not always from the sublime to the ridiculous: sometimes, as in "Nettles," she shows that the unattractive nettle can still nourish butterfly caterpillars. She carries this contrast between idealized and everyday reality further in another poem about a Japanese painting, "A Screen Depicting the Fifty-Four Episodes of the Tale of Genji on a Background of Gold Leaf." As he appears on the screen, Genji is a prince, a legendary lover, who progresses triumphantly from woman to woman in his glittering court. Real life, however, is different:

> A tea merchant of Kyoto commissioned this screen for his wife.
> At night as they lay on their uncomfortable mats
> she stared at it and sighed.
> He, however, concluded
> that the difference between his own life and Prince Genji's
> was that he lacked an artist
> to blot discreetly all but fifty-four moments
> with a dazzle of golden clouds.[51]

It is the artist who screens off uncomfortable reality from his golden fiction, and Pollitt is well aware both of the artist's deceit and of his or her genius. Pollitt herself is a miniaturist who captures elusive subjects with great delicacy and concision.

In contrast to some recent poems, Katha Pollitt's poems are unabashedly intelligent and often metaphysical. She majored in philosophy at Radcliffe and is intrigued by complexities and paradoxes, "the monochromatic / landscape of an ambiguous season: / hills neither gray nor green, / sky neither blue nor gray."[52] Although her poems are cerebral, they are firmly grounded in specific subjects, such as potatoes and onions. Indeed the number of her pastoral poems is surprising, since she grew up in Brooklyn and lives in Manhattan, working as a freelance writer. Her lines are graceful and quieter than those of many of her contemporaries, as if she were striving for a Japanese painter's "reticence, calm, clarity of mind."[53] So well-constructed are her poems that it is difficult to quote only a few lines without quoting the entire poem.

Pollitt combines her awareness of contraries and her intelligence with a vivid imagination that impels her best work toward that "Su-

preme Fiction" which was Wallace Stevens's goal. In the short space
of "A Turkish Story" she creates not only the setting of a distant culture, but also the contrasting emotions of those who live there:

> The rugweaver kept his daughters at home, unmarried.
> The soft clash of their bangles said *wish for us, wish*.
>
> Longing for a son, a handsome agronomist,
> for years he worked on a rug that would have no errors:
>
> the blue was disappointment, the red was rancor.
> His daughters circled their eyes with kohl and went to the market,
>
> they stirred pots, singing
> a song about a lion asleep under an almond tree.
>
> When he died each married a husband as strong as the sea.
> They danced on the rug, and its errors blazed like stars.[54]

In the future, hopefully, Katha Pollitt will succumb to her imagination even more, like the cultivated flowers she writes about in "Wild
Escapes," which seed themselves over the wall, where "a darker seed /
drove on a starker, more essential white."[55]

Peter Meinke sees a human being, and particularly the poet, as not
just one person, but a combination of four: "The Headman, the
Hunter, the Shaman and the Clown. . . . / four men are stalking
through the underbrush, they are in your blood. . . ."[56] As he describes them in "The Hunters: Southeast Africa," these four very different men work together to capture their game.

The Shaman, a magician who journeys in a trance, is a role
frequently assumed by poets, particularly in recent years. For Meinke,
this sometimes means a voyage to the inside of his own head, where
he discovers insane and even suicidal urges, and he wonders, "maybe
this is normal / to be half crazy."[57] Meinke realizes that others also
have mad impulses, except that

> Most people get lobotomies in middle age
> to ease the pain. They carve a hole in your head
> the size of a judge's fist, reach in and

> pull out the garbage: rats and raw nerves,
> lust and stinking hopes
> and that grinning devil with his unquenchable thirst
> and skin like sandpaper
> that scrapes you awake
> through those long Minneapolis nights [58]

The Clown is similar to the Shaman (who may also act crazy), yet in other ways the Clown contradicts the Shaman. While the Shaman is intensely serious, the Clown is witty and cynical and refuses to take anything seriously. Although Meinke can write uproariously comic poems, he is not merely a light-verse joker. In the East African hunting expedition Meinke describes, the Clown is brought along not to lead the way, or to perform magic, or to shoot their prey, but to observe, because "he will tell the story when they're done." [59] The Clown's function is to leaven reality with wit so we can bear it. Meinke's Clown tone often appears in his love poems, mocking their sentiment and making it believable. Sex, the lodestone of our times, is given full and funny exposure in Meinke's poems:

> you are what you eat & I
> I am a sexmad wheatgerm
> floating in holes of cheerios
> stamped out of Kansas farmland
> where in late August
> the All-American sun
> drives ripe farmgirls into barns [60]

The Clown balances the Shaman, and even saves him from self-destruction: "all my plans for suicide are ridiculous / I can never remember the heart's location." [61]

Meinke's poet also undertakes the role of Headman. This is unusual for contemporary poets, many of whom consider themselves outcasts. But Meinke is right in the thick of society and discovers in events which happen to ordinary people an effervescence which they are unable to articulate or sometimes even to realize. Even a casual Sunday drive to buy apples becomes a celebration of life.

> Apple-smell everywhere!
> Haralson   McIntosh   Fireside   Rome

old ciderpresses weathering in the shed
old ladders tilting at empty branches
boxes and bins of apples by the cartload
yellow and green and red
piled crazy in the storehouse barn
miraculous profusion, the crowd
around the testing table laughing and rolling
the cool applechunks in their mouths
dogs barking at children in the appletrees
couples holding hands, so many people
out in the country carrying bushels
and baskets and bags and boxes of apples
to their cars, the smell of apples
making us for one Sunday afternoon free
and happy as people must have been meant to be.[62]

As Headman of his family, Meinke finds some of his most joyful
moments with them. While his children play badminton in the sun,
he watches from behind air-conditioned glass with other weary adults;
then, "Are we in heaven? one asks, waking up / The answer, from the
children: Yes!"[63] Perhaps one of Meinke's most touching poems is
one written to his ten-year-old son, apologizing for having been angry
with him. Meinke's plain, conversational style is well suited to this
type of poem, which is able to say out loud some common truths that
tend to get overlooked in a world of junk and lies.

The Headman must also be the Hunter who provides, and
Meinke, stuck in a traffic jam on the way home from a fast-food expedition, has some bloodthirsty thoughts:

Today is our 16th anniversary
the suet anniversary, everything
turning to fat
At my side as I drive home squats Chicken Unlimited
the 16-piece box: we have four kids
sometimes I think we eat too much chicken
it makes us want to kill each other.[64]

Meinke the Hunter is a realist, and understands that not only family
life but civilization itself can be overshadowed by ancient, instinctual
savagery. Even in the ivory of sophisticated piano keys "the spirit of

captive elephant surrounds us."[65] The settings of Meinke's poems are often exotic—Africa, Eastern Europe—like the trophies brought back by a restless hunter.

And how does this four-sided poet Meinke has created fit into contemporary America? Sometimes he doesn't fit, like the undercover poetry lover J. Randall Randle who reads secretly in the rough on the golf course, or the poetry teacher struggling in a county school in Florida: "they're not bad kids. / Too dumb for poetry, and smart enough to know / they don't need it."[66] Yet the teacher persists, because he always manages to discover one brilliant embryo poet. The complementary and contradictory roles for the poet which Meinke has created means that he can both eulogize and challenge America. These multiple roles give Meinke's poems a bracing vitality and range.

These are but a few of the vigorous new poets writing at this moment, which is a good time for poetry. Now that the battle-smoke of the previous three decades has blown away, it is possible to write poetry which is not a reaction to any previous movements but which determines its own shape. The poetry of the coming years will arise from contemporary reality, from the poet's own inner vision and from the poet transcending the bounds of both. The next chapters are unbounded and will be written not only by poets and critics but, more than ever, by intelligent and adventurous readers.

Notes

1. IT'S TIME TO ASK QUESTIONS

1. Peter Martin, "An Annotated Bibliography of Selected Little Magazines," *Triquarterly* 43 (1978), p. 668.
2. Geoffrey Soar, "Little Mags. in Big Trouble . . . ," *University College of London Bulletin* 4, no. 12 (February 1979), pp. 6–8.
3. Aristotle, *Poetics* 8. 1451ª.
4. John Dryden, "Parallel of Poetry and Painting" (1695), in *Essays*, ed. W. P. Ker (Oxford: Oxford University Press, 1900), II:138.
5. William Wordsworth, *The Prose Works of William Wordsworth*, ed. W. J. B. Owen and J. W. Smyser (Oxford: Oxford University Press, 1974) I:148.
6. Charles Baudelaire, "Correspondances," *Oeuvres complètes*, ed. Y.-G. LeDantec (Paris: Bibliothèque de la Pléiade, 1946), I:87.
7. Ezra Pound, "A Retrospect," in *The Poetics of the New American Poetry*, ed. Donald Allen and Warren Tallman (New York: Grove Press, 1960) p. 36.
8. Archibald MacLeish, *New and Collected Poems* (Boston: Houghton Mifflin, 1976), p. 106.
9. Wallace Stevens, *Collected Poems* (London: Faber & Faber, 1955), p. 128.
10. Roland Barthes, "Criticism as Language," in *20th Century Literary Criticism*, ed. David Lodge (London: Longman, 1972), pp. 650, 651; italics mine.
11. Allen Ginsberg, "Notes for *Howl and Other Poems*," in *The New American Poetry*, ed. Donald Allen (New York: Grove Press, 1960) p. 417.

12. John Berryman, *His Toy, His Dream, His Rest* (London: Faber & Faber, 1964), p. 99.
13. Susan Sontag, "Against Interpretation," in Lodge, *op. cit.*, pp. 655–56.
14. Marcel Proust, *Remembrance of Things Past*, tr. C. K. Scott-Moncrieff (London: Chatto & Windus, 1966), I:9.
15. Charles Olson, in Allen, *op. cit.*, p. 388.
16. Ginsberg, *op. cit.*, p. 415.
17. Denise Levertov, in Allen and Tallman, *op. cit.*, p. 317.
18. Lenore Kandel, *Word Alchemy* (New York: Grove Press, 1960), p. v.
19. Dionysius Cassius Longinus, *On Sublimity*, tr. D. A. Russell (Oxford: Oxford University Press, 1965), p. 7.

2. STILL LIFE FROM A MIDDLE DISTANCE:
CONVENTIONAL POETS OF THE FIFTIES

1. W. K. Wimsatt, Jr., and M. C. Beardsley, "The Intentional Fallacy," in W. K. Wimsatt, Jr., *The Verbal Icon* (London: Methuen, 1970), p. 4.
2. John Crowe Ransom, "Criticism Inc.," in Lodge, *op. cit.*, p. 229.
3. Philip Larkin, *The Whitsun Weddings* (London: Faber & Faber, 1964), p. 22.
4. *Ibid.*
5. *Ibid.*, p. 38.
6. Philip Larkin, *The Less Deceived* (Hessle, East Yorkshire: Marvell Press, 1955), p. 32.
7. Philip Larkin, in *The London Magazine* 13, no. II (November 1956); *idem*, on BBC radio broadcast, as quoted in Anthony Thwaite, *Phoenix* 11/12 (1973–74), p. 47.
8. Larkin, *Whitsun Weddings*, p. 16.
9. Anthony Hartley, quoted by Ian Hamilton in *A Poetry Chronicle* (London: Faber & Faber, 1973), p. 129.
10. Philip Larkin, *All What Jazz?* (London: Faber & Faber, 1970), p. 1.
11. Philip Larkin, *High Windows* (London: Faber & Faber, 1974), p. 14.
12. Larkin, *Whitsun Weddings*, p. 46.
13. Quoted in Thwaite, *op. cit.*, p. 50.
14. Larkin, *Whitsun Weddings*, p. 30.
15. Larkin, *High Windows*, p. 14.
16. D. J. Enright, *The Laughing Hyena* (London: Routledge and Kegan Paul, 1953), p. 19.
17. *Ibid.*, pp. 20–21.
18. D. J. Enright, *Bread Rather Than Blossoms* (London: Secker & Warburg, 1956), p. 45.
19. D. J. Enright, *Sad Ires* (London: Chatto & Windus, 1975), p. 36.
20. D. J. Enright, *The Terrible Shears* (London: Chatto & Windus, 1973), p. 50.
21. *Ibid.*, p. 11.

22. Enright, *Sad Ires*, p. 33.
23. D. J. Enright, *Some Men Are Brothers* (London: Chatto & Windus, 1960), p. 46.
24. Richard Wilbur, *Advice to a Prophet* (London: Faber & Faber, 1962), pp. 15–17.
25. Richard Wilbur, *Walking to Sleep* (London: Faber & Faber, 1971), p. 44.
26. G. B. Deeping and Michel Francisque, *Wayland Smith* (London: William Pickering, 1847). See also C. S. Moncrieff, trans., *Widsith, Beowulf, Finnsburgh, Waldere, Deor* (London: Chapman & Hall, 1921).
27. Howard Nemerov, *The Blue Swallows* (Chicago: University of Chicago Press, 1967), p. 11.
28. Howard Nemerov, *The Next Room of the Dream* (Chicago: University of Chicago Press, 1962), p. 50.
29. Nemerov, *Blue Swallows*, p. 51.
30. Howard Nemerov, *New and Selected Poems* (Chicago: University of Chicago Press, 1962), p. 50.
31. R. Conquest, ed., *New Lines II* (London: Macmillan, 1963), p. xvi.
32. Nemerov, *Blue Swallows*, pp. 89–90.

3. "THE WILL TO CHANGE": THE BLACK MOUNTAIN POETS

1. Harold Bloom, *The Anxiety of Influence* (New York: Oxford University Press, 1973), p. 5.
2. To Cid Corman, July 24, 1951, *Letters for Origin* (London: Cape Goliard, 1969), p. 130.
3. To Robert Creeley, March 8, 1951, *Mayan Letters* (London: Cape Editions, 1968), p. 30.
4. Charles Olson, "Projective Verse," in Allen and Tallman, *op. cit.*, p. 149.
5. Marjorie Perloff, "Charles Olson and the 'Inferior Predecessors': 'Projective Verse' Revisited," in *English Literary History* (Baltimore: Johns Hopkins University Press, 1973), 40:295.
6. To Cid Corman, July 31, 1951, *Letters for Origin*, p. 69.
7. Olson, "Projective Verse," p. 149.
8. *Ibid.*, p. 148.
9. *Ibid.*, p. 150.
10. *Ibid.*, p. 156.
11. Charles Olson, *The Distances* (New York: Grove Press, 1960), p. 83.
12. Olson, "Projective Verse," p. 149.
13. Charles Olson, *The Maximus Poems, Volume Three* (New York: Grossman, 1975), p. 176.
14. Charles Olson, *Maximus Poems IV, V, VI* (London: Cape Goliard, 1968), unpaged; sheet 87b.
15. Olson, *Distances*, p. 68.
16. To Cid Corman, December 14, 1953, *Letters for Origin*, p. 133.
17. Robert Creeley, *The Finger* (London: Calder & Boyars, 1970), p. 106.

18. Robert Creeley, *Poems 1950–1965* (London: Calder & Boyars, 1966), p. 142.
19. *Ibid.*, p. 19.
20. *Ibid.*, p. 218–19.
21. *Ibid.*, p. 164.
22. Edward Dorn, *The Collected Poems, 1956–1974* (Bolinas, Calif.: Four Seasons Foundation, 1975), p. 222.
23. *Ibid.*, p. 23.
24. *Ibid.*, p. 218.
25. *Ibid.*, p. 226.
26. *Ibid.*, p. 233.
27. Denise Levertov, "An Admonition," in Allen and Tallman, *op. cit.*, p. 310.
28. Denise Levertov, *The Jacob's Ladder* (New York: New Directions, 1961), p. 21.
29. Denise Levertov, *With Eyes at the Back of Our Heads* (New York: New Directions, 1959), p. 16.
30. *Ibid.*, p. 9.
31. Denise Levertov, *The Freeing of the Dust* (New York: New Directions, 1975), p. 39.
32. Denise Levertov, *To Stay Alive* (New York: New Directions, 1971), p. 58.
33. Levertov, "An Admonition," p. 311.
34. Denise Levertov, *O Taste and See* (New York: New Directions, 1964), p. 71.
35. Levertov, *Freeing of the Dust*, p. 17.
36. Robert Duncan, *The Opening of the Field* (New York: Grove Press, 1960), p. 8.
37. Robert Duncan, *Bending the Bow* (New York: New Directions, 1968), p. 19.
38. Robert Duncan, *Roots and Branches* (New York: Charles Scribner's Sons, 1964), p. 42.
39. Duncan, *Opening of the Field*, p. 37.
40. Duncan, *Roots and Branches*, p. 45.
41. Robert Duncan, *The First Decade* (London: Fulcrum Press, 1968), pp. 113–14.
42. Duncan, *Opening of the Field*, p. 69.
43. Robert Duncan, Preface to *Letters* (Highlands, N.C.: Jargon, 1958), p. iii.
44. Duncan, *Opening of the Field*, p. 50.
45. Charles Olson, *The Distances* (New York: Grove Press, 1960), p. 5.

4. "WHITMAN'S WILD CHILDREN": THE BEATS

1. Allen Ginsberg, *Howl* (San Francisco: City Lights Books, 1956), p. 12.
2. Euripides, *The Bacchae*, tr. P. Vellacott (London: Penguin, 1964), p. 191.

3. Allen Ginsberg, *Allen Verbatim*, ed. G. Ball (New York: McGraw-Hill, 1974), p. 107.
4. Ginsberg, *Howl*, pp. 31, 33.
5. *Ibid.*, p. 24.
6. Allen Ginsberg, *Empty Mirror* (New York: Totem/Corinth Books, 1961), p. 19.
7. Ginsberg, "Notes for *Howl and Other Poems*," p. 318.
8. Ginsberg, *Howl*, p. 32.
9. Allen Ginsberg, *Kaddish* (San Francisco: City Lights Books, 1961), p. 22.
10. *Ibid.*, p. 100.
11. Ginsberg, "Notes for *Howl and Other Poems*," p. 318.
12. *Ibid.*, p. 345.
13. See Tosafot to the Babylonian Talmud tractate *Berachot* 3a.
14. Ginsberg, *Kaddish*, p. 33.
15. Allen Ginsberg, *Iron Horse* (San Francisco: City Lights Books, 1974), p. 13.
16. Ginsberg, "Notes for *Howl and Other Poems*," p. 320.
17. Allen Ginsberg, *Airplane Journals* (San Francisco: City Lights Books, 1968), p. 31.
18. Quoted by Eric Mottram, in *Allen Ginsberg in the Sixties* (Brighton: Unicorn Bookshop, 1972), p. 20.
19. Allen Ginsberg, " 'When the Mode of the Music Changes the Walls of the City Shake,' " in Allen and Tallman, *op. cit.*, p. 324.
20. *Ibid.*, p. 328.
21. Gregory Corso, *Gasoline* (San Francisco: City Lights Books, 1958), p. 46.
22. Gregory Corso, *The Happy Birthday of Death* (New York: New Directions, 1960), p. 30.
23. Gregory Corso, *Long Live Man* (New York: New Directions, 1962), p. 66.
24. Lawrence Ferlinghetti, *The Secret Meaning of Things* (New York: New Directions 1966), p. 33.
25. Lawrence Ferlinghetti, *Who Are We Now?* (New York: New Directions, 1976), p. 62.
26. *Ibid.*, p. 44.
27. Gary Snyder, *A Range of Poems* (London: Fulcrum, 1966), p. 29.
28. Gary Snyder quoted in Allen, *op. cit.*, p. 421.
29. Gary Snyder, *Regarding Wave* (New York: New Directions, 1970), p. 13.
30. *Ibid.*, p. 45.
31. *Ibid.*, pp. 52–53.
32. Saul Bellow, *Humbolt's Gift* (London: Secker & Warburg, 1975), pp. 117–18.
33. Mottram, Eric, "d. a. levy: Cleveland's Survival Artist," in *Serif* 8, no. 4 (Kent, Ohio: Kent State University Libraries, 1972), p. 6.
34. levy, d. a., *Suburban Monastery Death Poem* (Cleveland: Offense Fund Reprint, Zero Editions, 1976), p. 1.
35. Russell Atkins, "For Lev," *Serif* 8, no. 4 (1972), p. 21.
36. levy, *op. cit.*, 'pre-face.'
37. *Ibid.*, p. 1.

38. Quoted by Alex Gildzen, in "Editorial Notes," *Serif* 8, no. 4 (1972), p. 3.

39. levy, *op. cit.*, p. 21.

40. *Ibid.*, p. 4.

5. "ALONG THE RAZOR'S EDGE": THE EXTREMISTS

1. Robert Lowell, *Life Studies* (London: Faber & Faber, 1959), p. 54.

2. *Ibid.*, p. 60.

3. Quoted in George Plimpton, ed., *Writers at Work: The Paris Review Interviews, Second Series* (New York: Viking Press, 1963), p. 346.

4. Lowell, Robert, "91 Revere Street," *Partisan Review* 25 (Winter–Spring, 1961), p. 449. See also the U.S. edition of *Life Studies*, (New York: Farrar, Straus & Giroux, 1959).

5. Lowell, *Life Studies*, pp. 55–56.

6. *Ibid.*, pp. 40–41.

7. See *ibid.*, p. 59.

8. *Ibid.*, p. 53.

9. *Ibid.*, p. 35.

10. Ian Hamilton, "A Conversation with Robert Lowell," *The Review*, no. 26 (Summer 1971), p. 26.

11. Charles Newman, ed., *The Art of Sylvia Plath* (London: Faber & Faber, 1970), p. 194.

12. Sylvia Plath, *Letters Home*, ed. Aurelia Schober Plath (London: Faber & Faber, 1975), p. 487.

13. Sylvia Plath, *Ariel* (London: Faber & Faber, 1965), p. 60.

14. *Ibid.*, p. 62.

15. Sylvia Plath, *The Colossus* (London: Faber & Faber, 1960), p. 75.

16. *Ibid.*, p. 38.

17. Plath, *Ariel*, p. 66.

18. *Ibid.*, p. 50.

19. Plath, *Colossus*, p. 85.

20. Plath, *Ariel*, p. 49.

21. Richard Howard, *Alone with America* (London: Thames and Hudson, 1970), p. 416.

22. Phyllis Chesler, *Women and Madness* (London: Allen Lane, 1972), p. 12.

23. Plath, *Letters*, p. 498.

24. Plath, *Ariel*, p. 63.

25. Newman, *op. cit.*, pp. 280–82.

26. Plath, *Colossus*, p. 75.

27. Sylvia Plath, *The Winter Trees* (London: Faber & Faber, 1971), p. 37.

28. Plath, *Ariel*, p. 60.

29. *Ibid.*, p. 66.

30. *Ibid.*, pp. 66–67.

31. *Ibid.*, p. 69.

32. Quoted in Newman, *op. cit.*, p. 156.

33. W. D. Snodgrass, quoted in Robert Boyers, ed., *Contemporary Poetry in America* (New York: Schocken Books, 1974), p. 175.
34. W. D. Snodgrass, *Heart's Needle* (New York: Knopf, 1957), p. 65.
35. Rainer Maria Rilke, *Duino Elegies*, tr. J. B. Leishman and Stephen Spender (New York: Norton, 1939), p. 77 (no. 9, l. 64).
36. Snodgrass, *Heart's Needle*, p. 19.
37. W. D. Snodgrass, *After Experience* (New York: Oxford University Press, 1968), p. 6.
38. *Ibid.*, p. 9.
39. *Ibid.*, pp. 16, 17.
40. Snodgrass, *Heart's Needle*, p. 45.
41. *Ibid.*, p. 63.
42. *Ibid.*, p. 74.
43. P. Leary and R. Kelly, eds., *A Controversy of Poets* (New York: Doubleday & Co., 1965), p. 550.
44. Snodgrass, *Heart's Needle*, p. 55.
45. Quoted in George Plimpton, ed., *Writers at Work: The Paris Review Interviews, Fourth Series* (London: Secker & Warburg, 1977), p. 308.
46. John Berryman, *His Toy, His Dream, His Rest* (London: Faber & Faber, 1969), p. 200.
47. *Ibid.*, p. 259.
48. John Berryman, *77 Dream Songs* (London: Faber & Faber, 1964), p. 3.
49. Berryman, *His Toy, His Dream, His Rest*, p. 11.
50. Quoted in Plimpton, *Writers at Work, Fourth Series*, p. 322.
51. John Berryman, *Love and Fame* (London: Faber & Faber, 1971), p. 71.
52. Berryman, *77 Dream Songs*, p. 46.
53. Berryman, *His Toy, His Dream, His Rest*, p. 4.
54. *Ibid.*, p. 316.

6. "NEON IN DAYLIGHT": THE NEW YORK POETS

1. Frank O'Hara, *Collected Poems* (New York: Knopf, 1972), pp. 257–58.
2. See Hans Richter, *Dada: Art and Anti-Art* (London: Thames and Hudson, 1965), quoting Breton, p. 194.
3. John Ashbery, in *The Craft of Poetry*, ed. William Packard (New York: Doubleday, 1974), p. 124.
4. O'Hara, *op. cit.*, p. 332.
5. O'Hara, *op. cit.*, p. 332.
6. *Ibid.*, p. 512.
7. *Ibid.*, p. 49.
8. *Ibid.*, p. 499.
9. *Ibid.*, p. 350.
10. *Ibid.*, p. 224.
11. *Ibid.*, p. 387.
12. *Ibid.*, p. 199.
13. *Ibid.*, p. 197.

14. *Ibid.*, pp. 349–50.
15. *Ibid.*, p. 168.
16. John Ashbery, *Rivers and Mountains* (New York: The Ecco Press, 1977), pp. 10, 11. In the U.K. see *Selected Poems* (London: Cape, 1967), pp. 23, 24.
17. O'Hara, *op. cit.*, p. 498.
18. Ashbery, *Rivers and Mountains*, p. 34.
19. *Ibid.*, p. 52.
20. See John Ashbery, *Self-Portrait in a Convex Mirror* (New York: Viking, 1975), p. 46.
21. John Ashbery, *Three Poems* (New York: Viking, 1972), p. 3.
22. Ashbery, *Rivers and Mountains*, p. 39.
23. See Ashbery, *Self-Portrait in a Convex Mirror*, p. 61.
24. Quoted in Richard Howard, *Alone with America* (London: Thames and Hudson, 1970), pp. 29–30.
25. See Ashbery, *Self-Portrait in a Convex Mirror*, p. 24.
26. *Ibid.*, p. 69.
27. Ashbery, *Rivers and Mountains*, p. 41.
28. *Ibid.*, pp. 42, 43.
29. *Ibid.*, p. 38.
30. Ashbery, *Self-Portrait in a Convex Mirror*, p. 70.
31. *Ibid.*, p. 74.
32. *Ibid.*, p. 78.
33. Ashbery, *Rivers and Mountains*, pp. 42, 56, 59, 60.
34. *Ibid.*, pp. 37–38.
35. John Ashbery, quoted in David Kalstone, *Five Temperaments* (New York: Oxford University Press, 1977), p. 174.
36. Ashbery, *Rivers and Mountains*, p. 50.
37. Kenneth Koch, *Thank You and Other Poems* (New York: Grove Press, 1962), p. 77.
38. *Ibid.*, p. 68.
39. *Ibid.*, p. 56.
40. James Schuyler, *The Crystal Lithium* (New York: Random House, 1972), p. 39.
41. *Ibid.*, p. 9.
42. *Ibid.*, p. 11.
43. *Ibid.*, p. 55.
44. *Ibid.*, p. 80.
45. *Ibid.*, pp. 87–89.

7. THE AMERICAN BLUE TOAD SWALLOWS A SPANISH FLY

1. *The Fifties*, no. 3 (1959), p. 57.
2. Pablo Neruda, *Selected Poems*, ed. and tr. Ben Belitt (New York: Grove Press, 1961), p. 39.
3. *The Sixties*, no. 4 (Fall 1960), p. 3.

4. *El Corno Emplumado*, no. 26 (April 1968), p. 6.
5. *The Sixties*, no. 7 (Winter 1964), p. 18.
6. Robert Bly, ed., *Forty Poems Touching on Recent American History* (Boston: Beacon Press, 1970), p. 10.
7. Robert Bly, *The Morning Glory* (San Francisco: Kayak Books, 1969), p. 21.
8. Robert Bly, *Sleepers Joining Hands* (New York: Harper & Row, 1973), p. 6.
9. *Ibid.*, p. 50.
10. Nathan Silverstein, "On James Dickey," in *Contemporary Poetry in America*, ed. Robert Boyers (New York: Schocken Books, 1974), p. 312.
11. James Dickey, *Poems 1957–1967* (London: Rapp & Carroll, 1967), p. 279.
12. James Dickey, *The Eye-Beaters, Blood, Victory, Madness, Buckhead and Mercy* (London: Hamish Hamilton, 1971), p. 7.
13. Dickey, *Poems 1957–1967*, p. 21.
14. *Ibid.*, p. 100.
15. Dickey, *The Eye-Beaters*, p. 12.
16. Dickey, *Poems 1957–1967*, p. 184.
17. *The Sixties*, no. 9 (Spring 1967), p. 79.
18. Dickey, *Poems 1957–1967*, p. 186.
19. Robert Bly, *The Teeth Mother Naked at Last* (San Francisco: City Lights Books, 1970), p. 13.
20. Dickey, *Poems 1957–1967*, p. 184.
21. *Ibid.*, p. 181.
22. *The Sixties*, no. 9 (Spring 1967), pp. 70, 71.
23. Dickey, *Poems 1957–1967*, p. 123.
24. *Ibid.*, p. 126.
25. Sidney Lanier, *Poems of Sidney Lanier* (New York: Charles Scribner's Sons, 1903), p. 18.
26. Dickey, *Poems 1957–1967*, p. 108.
27. *Ibid.*, pp. 119–20.
28. Quoted in Silverstein, *op. cit.*, p. 306.
29. James Wright, *Two Citizens* (New York: Farrar, Straus and Giroux, 1973), p. 45.
30. James Wright, *Collected Poems* (Middletown, Conn.: Wesleyan University Press, 1971), p. 154.
31. *Ibid.*, p. 78.
32. *Ibid.*, p. 119.
33. *Ibid.*, p. 139.
34. *Ibid.*, p. 136.
35. Wright, *Two Citizens*, p. 58.
36. Wright, *Collected Poems*, p. 134.
37. William Stafford, *Traveling Through the Dark* (New York: Harper & Row, 1962), p. 93.
38. *Ibid.*, p. 30.
39. *Ibid.*, p. 79.

40. *Ibid.*, p. 59.
41. *Ibid.*, p. 29.
42. *Ibid.*, p. 75.
43. *Ibid.*, p. 67.
44. Lorine Niedecker, *Collected Poems 1936–1968* (London: Fulcrum, 1970), p. 33. Niedecker's *Selected Poems* will be published in a definitive edition by Jargon Press (Highlands, N.C.) in fall 1981.
45. *Ibid.*, p. 20.
46. *Ibid.*, p. 66.
47. *Ibid.*, p. 76.
48. Louis Simpson, *Adventures of the Letter I* (London: Oxford University Press, 1971), p. 42.
49. Louis Simpson, *At the End of the Open Road* (Middletown, Conn.: Wesleyan University Press, 1963), p. 36.
50. Simpson, *Adventures of the Letter I*, p. 56.
51. Simpson, *At the End of the Open Road*, pp. 64–65.
52. Louis Simpson, *Searching for the Ox* (London: Oxford University Press, 1976), p. 27.
53. Simpson, *At the End of the Open Road*, p. 69.
54. Simpson, *Searching for the Ox*, p. 12.
55. *Ibid.*, p. 43.
56. *Ibid.*, p. 52.
57. Galway Kinnell, *What a Kingdom It Was* (Boston: Houghton Mifflin, 1960), p. 83.
58. Galway Kinnell, *Flower Herding on Mount Monadnock* (Boston: Houghton Mifflin, 1964), p. 45.
59. Galway Kinnell, *The Book of Nightmares* (Boston: Houghton Mifflin, 1971), p. 8.
60. *Ibid.*, p. 59.

8. "THE VOYAGE OF RECOVERY": RECENT BRITISH POETRY

1. David Wright, ed., *The Mid Century: English Poetry 1940–60* (London: Penguin, 1965), p. 17.
2. Stephen Berg and Robert Mezey, eds., *Naked Poetry* (Indianapolis and New York: Bobbs-Merrill, 1969), p. xii.
3. Simpson, *At the End of the Open Road*, p. 68.
4. Donald Davie, *Thomas Hardy and British Poetry* (London: Routledge and Kegan Paul, 1973), p. 184.
5. Charles Tomlinson, *Written on Water* (London: Oxford University Press, 1972), p. 50.
6. Geoffrey Hill, *Mercian Hymns* (London: Andre Deutsch, 1971), no. I.
7. *Ibid.*, no. XX.
8. *Ibid.*, no. XIII.
9. *Ibid.*, no. XXV.
10. *Ibid.*, no. V.

11. *Ibid.*, no. XXIII.
12. *Ibid.*, no. XXIII.
13. *Ibid.*, no. XXIII.
14. Ted Hughes, quoted in *Worlds*, ed. Geoffrey Summerfield (London: Penguin, 1974), p. 122.
15. Ted Hughes, *Crow* (London: Faber and Faber, 1970), p. 13.
16. Ted Hughes, *Wodwo* (London: Faber and Faber, 1967), p. 34.
17. Hughes, *Crow*, p. 19.
18. Peter Redgrove, *At the White Monument* (London: Routledge and Kegan Paul, 1963), p. 20.
19. Peter Redgrove, *Dr. Faust's Sea-Spiral Spirit* (London: Routledge and Kegan Paul, 1972), p. 25.
20. Peter Redgrove, *The Nature of Cold Weather* (London: Routledge and Kegan Paul, 1961), p. 8.
21. Redgrove, *At the White Monument*, p. 19.
22. Charles Tomlinson, *American Scenes* (London: Oxford University Press, 1966), p. 44.
23. Charles Tomlinson, *A Peopled Landscape* (London: Oxford University Press, 1963), p. 4.
24. Charles Tomlinson, *The Way In* (London: Oxford University Press, 1974), p. 5.
25. *Ibid.*, p. 5.
26. *Ibid.*, p. 8.
27. *Ibid.*, p. 40.
28. Tomlinson, *American Scenes*, p. 34.
29. Tomlinson, *The Way In*, p. 10.
30. Tomlinson, *Written on Water*, p. 8.
31. *Ibid.*, p. 50.
32. R. S. Thomas, *Selected Poems* (London: Hart-Davis MacGibbon, 1973), p. 9.
33. *Ibid.*, p. 117.
34. *Ibid.*, p. 10.
35. Edwin Morgan, *The Second Life* (Edinburgh: Edinburgh University Press, 1968), p. 37.
36. *Ibid.*, p. 44.
37. Edwin Morgan, quoted in Summerfield, *op. cit.*, p. 229.
38. Seamus Heaney, *Wintering Out* (London: Faber and Faber, 1972), p. 25.
39. Seamus Heaney, *Death of a Naturalist* (London: Faber and Faber, 1966), p. 23.
40. Heaney, *Wintering Out*, p. 48.
41. Seamus Heaney, *North* (London: Faber and Faber, 1975), p. 60.
42. *Ibid.*, p. 70.
43. *Ibid.*, p. 73.
44. *Ibid.*, 65.
45. Heaney, *Wintering Out*, p. 31.
46. Heaney, *North*, p. 59.
47. A. Alvarez, *Autumn to Autumn* (London: Macmillan, 1978), p. 11.

48. Roy Fisher, *Poems 1955–1980* (Oxford: Oxford University Press, 1980), p. 23.
49. *Ibid.*, p. 17.

9. "WE SAY, TODAY. THIS DAY.": NEW POETS

1. Jordan Smith, "Sugar in the Gourd" (ms., 1978), p. 39. "Vine Valley" appeared in *The Agni Review* 12.
2. *Ibid.*, p. 20.
3. *Ibid.*, p. 11. "Kossow's, The Cottage Hotel, and the Rock" appeared in *Shenandoah* 29 (Spring 1978).
4. Jordan Smith, "The Immigrant's Stars," in *The Ardis Anthology of New American Poetry*, ed. David Rigsbee and Ellendea Proffer (Ann Arbor, Mich.: Ardis, 1977), p. 298.
5. Smith, "Vine Valley."
6. Smith, "Sugar in the Gourd," in ms. of the same title, p. 22.
7. *Ibid.*, p. 21.
8. Smith, "Inheritance," in "Sugar in the Gourd," p. 26.
9. Smith, "The Oxbow," in "Sugar in the Gourd," pp. 41, 42, 43, 44.
10. Craig Raine, *A Martian Sends a Postcard Home* (Oxford: Oxford University Press, 1979), p. 1.
11. Craig Raine, *The Onion, Memory* (Oxford: Oxford University Press, 1978), p. 16.
12. *Ibid.*, p. 62.
13. *Ibid.*, p. 10.
14. *Ibid.*, p. 22.
15. Raine, *A Martian Sends a Postcard Home*, p. 24.
16. *Ibid.*, p. 24.
17. Raine, *The Onion, Memory*, p. 42.
18. Raine, *A Martian Sends a Postcard Home*, p. 14.
19. *Ibid.*, p. 1.
20. Letter to RB, February 1979.
21. Lynn Strongin, "Multiplication," in Rigsbee and Proffer, *op. cit.*, p. 197.
22. Lynn Strongin, *A Hacksaw Brightness* (Tucson: Ironwood Press, 1977), p. 9.
23. Lynn Strongin, *Nightmare of Mouse* (Fort Collins, Colo.: L'Epervier Press, 1977), p. 55.
24. *Ibid.*, p. 38.
25. Letter to RB, February 1979.
26. Strongin, *Nightmare of Mouse*, p. 15.
27. Letter to RB, February 1979.
28. Rolly Kent, "In Grandmother's Room," in "Blue House" (ms., 1979), p. 11.
29. Letter to RB, February 1979.
30. Rolly Kent, "The Wreck in Post Office Canyon," in "Blue House," pp. 34, 35.

31. Letter to RB, February 1979.
32. Rolly Kent, "For Friends," in "Blue House," p. 55, 56.
33. Alex Gildzen, *The Year Book* (Plainfield, Vt.: North Atlantic Books, 1974), unpaged, but dated: 18 sept.: Monterey.
34. *Ibid.*, 3 dec: TL.
35. *Ibid.*, 22 june: K.
36. *Ibid.*, 21 nov: TL.
37. *Ibid.*, 29 jan: TL.
38. *Ibid.*, 20 feb: TL.
39. *Ibid.*, 27 june: TL.
40. Letter to RB, June 1976.
41. Alex Gildzen, *New Notes* (Kent, Ohio: Shelly's Press, 1978), unpaged.
42. Calvin Hernton, *Medicine Man* (New York: Reed, Cannon & Johnson, 1976), p. 71.
43. *Ibid.*, p. 63.
44. *Ibid.*, p. 98.
45. *Ibid.*, p. 100.
46. *Ibid.*, p. 47.
47. *Ibid.*, p. 90.
48. Jones, LeRoi, "How You Sound??" in *The New American Poetry*, ed. Donald Allen (New York: Grove Press, 1960), p. 424.
49. Hernton, *op. cit.*, pp. 109, 113, 114.
50. *The New Yorker*, March 14, 1977.
51. *Poetry* (Chicago), forthcoming.
52. Katha Pollitt, "Discussion of the Vicissitudes of History Under a Pine Tree," *The New Yorker*, March 13, 1978.
53. Katha Pollitt, "Wild Orchids," *The New Yorker*, March 14, 1977.
54. *The Nation*, May 17, 1975.
55. *Paris Review* 77 (Winter–Spring 1980).
56. Peter Meinke, *Trying to Surprise God* (Pittsburgh: University of Pittsburgh Press, 1981).
57. Peter Meinke, *The Night Train and the Golden Bird* (Pittsburgh: University of Pittsburgh Press, 1977), p. 54.
58. *Ibid.*, p. 56.
59. Meinke, *Trying to Surprise God.*
60. Meinke, *Night Train and the Golden Bird*, p. 43.
61. *Ibid.*, p. 41.
62. *Ibid.*, p. 50.
63. Meinke, *Trying to Surprise God.*
64. Meinke, *Night Train and the Golden Bird*, p. 17.
65. Meinke, *Trying to Surprise God.*
66. Meinke, *Night Train and the Golden Bird*, p. 62.

Index

Copyrights and Acknowledgments